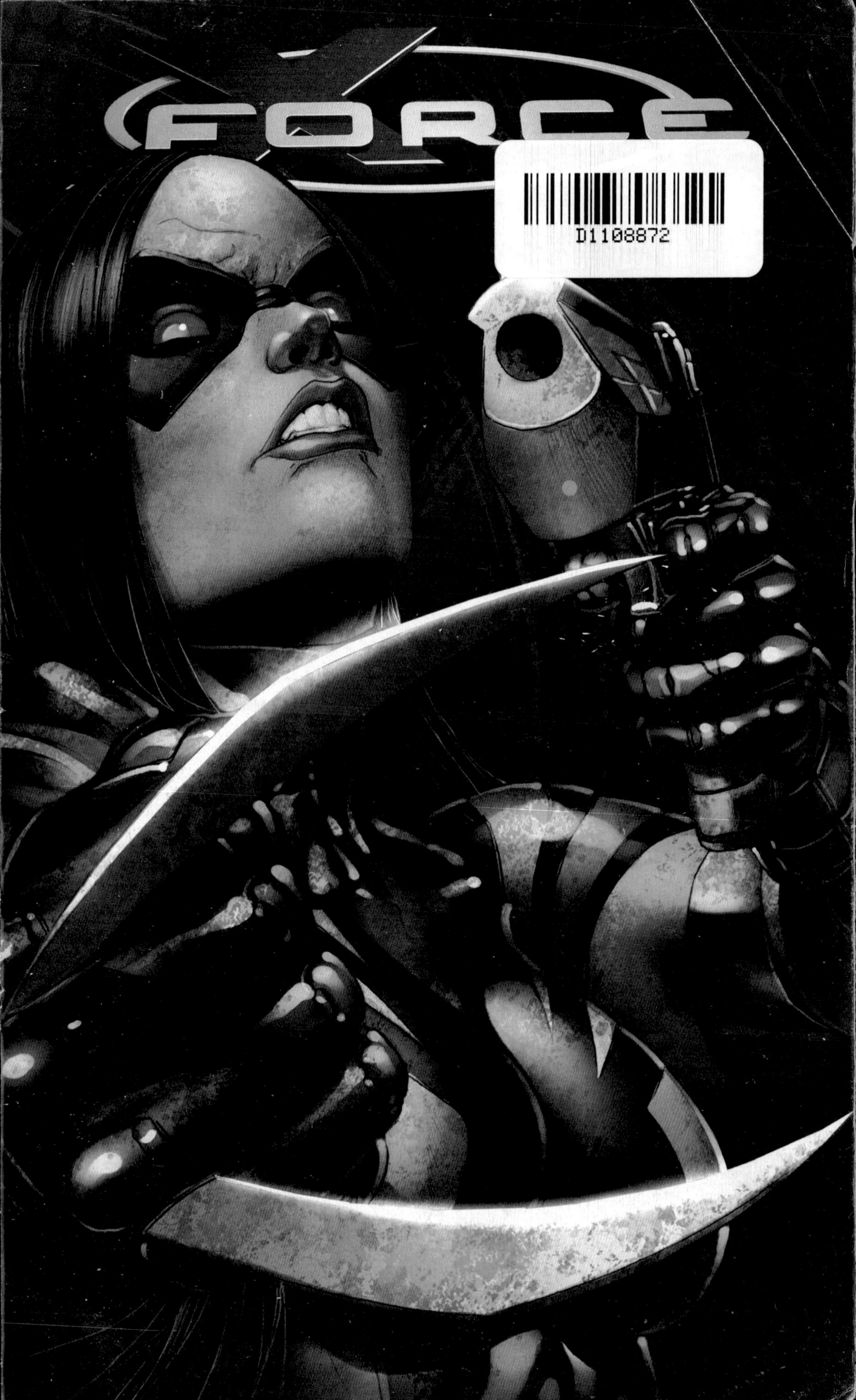
FORCE

COLLECTION EDITOR: JENNIFER GRÜNWALD • ASSOCIATE MANAGING EDITOR: ALEX STARBUCK • EDITOR, SPECIAL PROJECTS: MARK D. BEAZLEY
SENIOR EDITOR, SPECIAL PROJECTS: JEFF YOUNGQUIST • SVP PRINT, SALES & MARKETING: DAVID GABRIEL

EDITOR IN CHIEF: AXEL ALONSO • CHIEF CREATIVE OFFICER: JOE QUESADA • PUBLISHER: DAN BUCKLEY • EXECUTIVE PRODUCER: ALAN FINE

X-FORCE BY CRAIG KYLE & CHRIS YOST: THE COMPLETE COLLECTION VOL. 1. Contains material originally published in magazine form as X-FORCE #1-13, X-FORCE SPECIAL: AIN'T NO DOG ONE-SHOT a
X-FORCE ANNUAL #1. First printing 2014. ISBN# 978-0-7851-8966-4. Published by MARVEL WORLDWIDE, INC., a subsidiary of MARVEL ENTERTAINMENT, LLC. OFFICE OF PUBLICATION: 135 West 50th Street, N
York, NY 10020. **Printed in the U.S.A.** ALAN FINE, EVP - Office of the President, Marvel Worldwide, Inc. and EVP & CMO Marvel Characters B.V.; DAN BUCKLEY, Publis
& President - Print, Animation & Digital Divisions; JOE QUESADA, Chief Creative Officer; TOM BREVOORT, SVP of Publishing; DAVID BOGART, SVP of Operations & Procurement, Publishing; C.B. CEBULSKI, SVP
Creator & Content Development; DAVID GABRIEL, SVP of Print & Digital Publishing Sales; JIM O'KEEFE, VP of Operations & Logistics; DAN CARR, Executive Director of Publishing Technology; SUSAN CRESPI, Edito
Operations Manager; ALEX MORALES, Publishing Operations Manager; STAN LEE, Chairman Emeritus. For information regarding advertising in Marvel Comics or on Marvel.com, please contact Niza Disla, Direc
of Marvel Partnerships, at ndisla@marvel.com. For Marvel subscription inquiries, please call 800-217-9158. **Manufactured between 1/3/2014 and 2/10/2014 by QUAD/GRAPHICS, VERSAILLES, KY, US**

10 9 8 7 6 5 4 3 2 1

BY

CRAIG KYLE & CHRIS YOST

X-FORCE #1-6 & #12-13
ARTIST: CLAYTON CRAIN
LETTERER: VC'S CORY PETIT
COVER ART: CLAYTON CRAIN

X-FORCE #7-10
ARTIST: MIKE CHOI
COLOR ARTIST: SONIA OBACK
LETTERER: VC'S CORY PETIT
COVER ART: MIKE CHOI & SONIA OBACK

X-FORCE #11
ARTISTS: ALINA URUSOV
WITH CLAYTON CRAIN
LETTERER: VC'S CORY PETIT
COVER ART: CLAYTON CRAIN

X-FORCE SPECIAL: AIN'T NO DOG #1

"AIN'T NO DOG"
WRITER: CHARLIE HUSTON
ARTIST: JEFTE PALO
COLOR ARTIST: LEE LOUGHRIDGE
LETTERER: BLAMBOT'S NATE PIEKOS

"HUNTERS & KILLERS"
WRITER: JASON AARON
PENCILER: WERTHER DELL'EDERA
INKER: ANTONIO FUSO
COLOR ARTIST: ANDREW CROSSLEY
LETTERER: BLAMBOT'S NATE PIEKOS

COVER ART: BRYAN HITCH & PAUL MOUNTS

X-FORCE ANNUAL #1
WRITER: ROBERT KIRKMAN
ARTIST: JASON PEARSON
COLORIST: DAVE STEWART
LETTERER: JEFF ECKLEBERRY
COVER ART: JASON PEARSON & DAVE STEWART

ASSISTANT EDITORS: JODY LEHEUP, MIKE HORWITZ, AUBREY SITTERSON & SEBASTIAN GIRNER
EDITORS: JEANINE SCHAEFER & JOHN BARBER • EXECUTIVE EDITOR: AXEL ALONSO

M-Day cut the mutant population down from millions to just under two hundred. Since that day, mutants had suffered deaths but not a single birth. But hope returned...in the form of an infant girl.

The mutant-fearing religious sect called the Purifiers reached the mutant child just days after she was born. They burned her city to the ground and killed every man, woman, and child they could find in an attempt to destroy the girl they believed to be the mutant Antichrist.

The X-Men's leader, CYCLOPS, assembled a strike team who would do whatever it took to save the infant and stop the Purifiers. This team was composed of the X-Men's best trackers and killers and was designed to cross the lines that X-Men wouldn't.

The team was led by WOLVERINE and called X-FORCE.

They succeeded in saving the baby but at a high cost. The alien Hepzibah was severely injured and the mutant Caliban lost his life. Since the completion of their mission, the Purifiers have gone back into hiding and the remaining members of X-Force have scattered...

Until now.

1

ANGEL'S AERIE, THE COLORADO ROCKY MOUNTAINS.
IF YOU'D ASKED ME TWO MONTHS AGO IF I'D EVER BEEN TO COLORADO, I WOULD HAVE SAID, "NO." YOU SEE, MOST OF MY PAST WAS A MYSTERY TO ME.
MY MEMORIES WERE ERASED BY A MAD SCIENTIST WHO HAD A NASTY BEDSIDE MANNER AND TWISTED IDEAS ON HOW WEAPONS ARE MADE.

RECENTLY, I GOT MY MEMORIES BACK AND IT WAS LIKE WAKING UP FROM A LONG NIGHT OF DRINKING: THE STUFF YOU CAN REMEMBER IS ALL PRETTY GOOD.
IT'S THE PARTS OF THE NIGHT YOU'D RATHER NOT KNOW ABOUT THAT YOU FIND OUT FROM YOUR FRIENDS THE NEXT DAY.

BEFORE I GOT MY MEMORIES BACK, I CONSTANTLY SEARCHED FOR CLUES TO MY MISSING PAST. I WANTED TO KNOW WHERE I CAME FROM, WHAT I'D DONE, AND WHAT I'D LOST.
I NEEDED TO KNOW WHO I WAS AND WHO I REALLY AM.

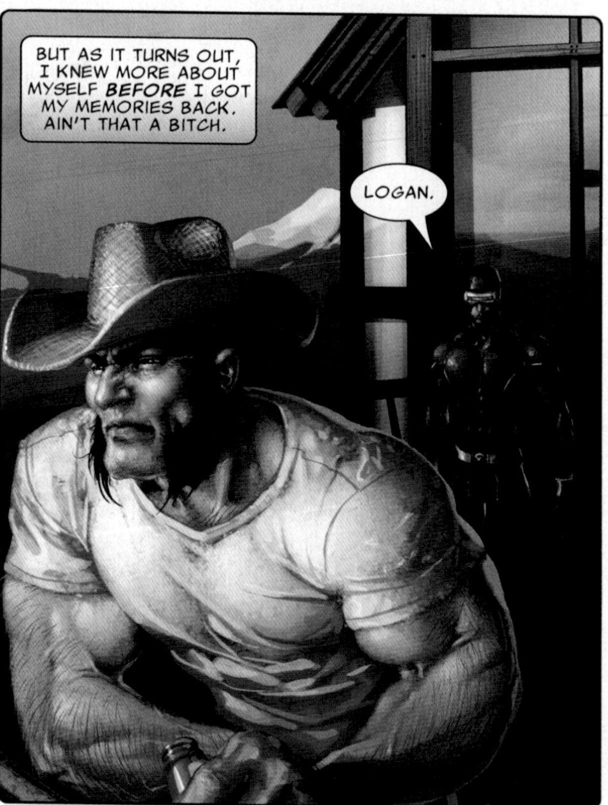
BUT AS IT TURNS OUT, I KNEW MORE ABOUT MYSELF BEFORE I GOT MY MEMORIES BACK. AIN'T THAT A BITCH.
LOGAN.

WHAT'S SINCLAIR DOING HERE? I THOUGHT YOU WANTED TO HAVE THIS LITTLE TALK IN PRIVATE.
I DO. RAHNE IS HERE BECAUSE...WELL, IT'S COMPLICATED.
OKAY. SO WHY AM I HERE?
SEVENTEEN HOURS AGO, A MAN TURNED HIMSELF IN TO A NORTH DAKOTA S.H.I.E.L.D. FACILITY...
"REVEREND MATTHEW RISMAN, LEADER OF THE PURIFIERS."
HE JUST GAVE HIMSELF UP?
WE'RE STILL FINDING OUT MORE DETAILS, BUT HERE'S WHAT WE KNOW SO FAR...

"HE MARCHED INTO THE BASE AND TOLD THE AGENTS HE WANTED TO CONFESS HIS SINS."
LATCHAM? WHAT ARE YOU DOING? I THOUGHT YOU WERE TRANSPORTING A PRISONER, I--
"BUT IT TURNS OUT, HE WAS JUST THERE TO COMMIT MORE OF THEM."
OH, GOD... LATCHAM, WHAT ARE YOU THINKING? YOU CAN'T BRING A PRISONER INTO THIS AREA!
GET THAT GUY OUT OF HERE!
"APPARENTLY, RISMAN HAD A PURIFIER WORKING INSIDE THE FACILITY."
I'M SORRY YOU PULLED ARMORY DETAIL TONIGHT, JOSH.
WHAT ARE YOU TALKING ABOUT? WHO ARE THESE GUYS, I DON'T RECOGNIZE--
THP! THP!
"LESS THAN AN HOUR AFTER HE TURNED HIMSELF IN, HE AND HIS MEN KILLED 16 S.H.I.E.L.D. AGENTS."
GOD HAVE MERCY ON YOUR SOUL.

"WILLIAM STRYKER AND HIS PURIFIERS KILLED MORE STUDENTS IN A SINGLE NIGHT THAN WE'VE LOST IN ALL THE YEARS SINCE THE XAVIER INSTITUTE'S DOORS FIRST OPENED.
"BUT STRYKER AND HIS PURIFIERS HAVE ALWAYS TARGETED MUTANTS.
"XAVIER, THE X-MEN, THE STUDENTS, THE BABY...
"FOR RISMAN TO ATTACK HUMANS...TO STAGE AN ASSAULT ON A S.H.I.E.L.D. FACILITY...THIS IS AN ESCALATION IN HIS ACTIONS LIKE NOTHING WE'VE EVER SEEN.
"NOW, IT SEEMS LIKELY THAT THE PURIFIERS HAVE SEVERAL HIGH-RANKING MEMBERS INSIDE THE GOVERNMENT, WHICH IS WHY S.H.I.E.L.D. IGNORED THE PURIFIERS' ATTACK ON THE MANSION.
"THIS ALSO EXPLAINS WHY THEY DIDN'T ACT ON THE ATTACK AT THE HOSPITAL IN ALASKA.
070109
"BUT THIS IS SOMETHING S.H.I.E.L.D. CAN'T IGNORE, NO MATTER HOW MANY MEN THE PURIFIERS HAVE ON THE INSIDE."
SO WHY'D HE DO IT?

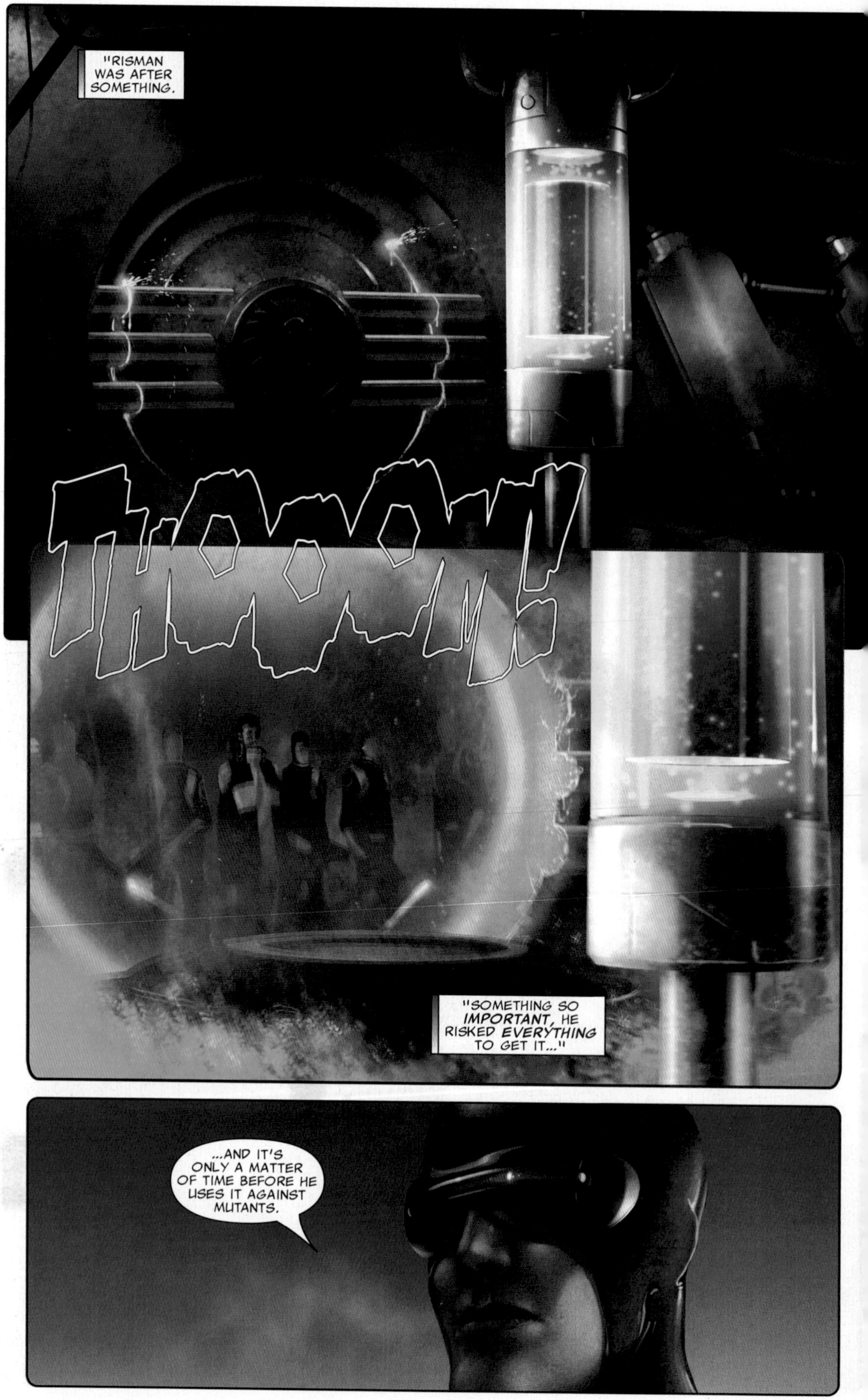

"RISMAN WAS AFTER SOMETHING.

THOOOM!

"SOMETHING SO ***IMPORTANT,*** HE RISKED ***EVERYTHING*** TO GET IT..."

...AND IT'S ONLY A MATTER OF TIME BEFORE HE USES IT AGAINST MUTANTS.

WELL, IF THOSE NUT-JOBS ARE DUMB ENOUGH TO COME AFTER US AGAIN, WE'LL TAKE 'EM DOWN. HARD.
NO. NOT THIS TIME.
I'M NOT WILLING TO WAIT UNTIL THERE ARE MORE DEAD MUTANTS ON OUR DOORSTEP.
NO, YOU'RE GOING AFTER RISMAN AND HIS PURIFIERS BEFORE THEY GET A CHANCE TO DO WHATEVER IT IS THEY HAVE PLANNED. AND WHEN YOU FIND THEM, YOU'RE GOING TO ELIMINATE THIS THREAT PERMANENTLY.
BUT YOU'RE NOT GOING IN ALONE. I WANT YOU TO PUT X-FORCE BACK TOGETHER.
DAMN, SUMMERS. I DON'T KNOW IF I SHOULD BE IMPRESSED, OR WORRIED YOU'VE SNAPPED.
WHAT'S FROST SAY ABOUT ALL THIS?
EMMA... DOESN'T NEED TO KNOW.
OKAY, I'M IMPRESSED.
DOESN'T MATTER, THOUGH. THERE IS NO X-FORCE, NOT ANYMORE. AFTER THE PURIFIERS KILLED CALIBAN, PROUDSTAR WENT M.I.A.
NO, HE DIDN'T. I KNOW WHERE HE IS.

OUTSIDE CAMP VERDE, ARIZONA.
BEING AN X-MAN...IT TOOK YOU FROM ME, JOHNNY. IT'S TAKEN SO MUCH, AND ALL IT'S LEFT ME IS A LEGACY I'VE FAILED TO LIVE UP TO.
I BURIED YOU HERE. I BURIED OUR ENTIRE TRIBE IN THE SHADOW OF YOUR GRAVE.
AND NOW HERE I AM AGAIN, PUTTING SOMEONE ELSE, SOMEONE I CARED ABOUT, BESIDE YOU.
YOU COULD HAVE SAVED HIM, JOHNNY...YOU COULD HAVE SAVED THEM ALL.
I NEED YOU HERE. I NEED YOU TO TEACH ME, TO GUIDE ME ON MY QUEST.
PLEASE FORGIVE ME.
SHK!
HNN!
AND IF CALIBAN IS WITH YOU, TELL HIM THAT I'M SORRY. I'M SORRY HE DIED FOR ME.
BUT I CAN GIVE HIS SPIRIT VENGEANCE.

I SWEAR THIS BLOOD OATH TO YOU...
...THE PURIFIERS WILL DIE.

WITH OR WITHOUT X-FORCE, ***WARPATH*** IS GOING AFTER THE PURIFIERS.

AND X-23 IS--

STOP.

STOP RIGHT THERE. IF JIMMY WANTS IN, THAT'S HIS DECISION. HE'S MAKING THAT CHOICE.

BUT LAURA DOESN'T KNOW ***HOW*** TO CHOOSE.

I BROUGHT HER TO XAVIER'S SO SHE COULD START A ***NEW LIFE,*** LEARN HOW TO BE A REAL PERSON. EVEN AFTER EVERYTHING THAT WENT DOWN WITH THE KIDS, I'M NOT GOING TO ASK HER TO KILL AGAIN.

FORGET IT.

YOU DON'T HAVE TO ASK HER.

I ALREADY ***DID.***

"SHE'S INSIDE THE S.H.I.E.L.D. FACILITY RIGHT NOW."
ONE ENTRANCE, ONE EXIT, SOUTHERN WALL. S.H.I.E.L.D. ARMORY, SEVEN WEAPONS MISSING, HIGH-VELOCITY RIFLES WITH EXPLOSIVE ROUNDS.
ONE DEAD, WHITE MALE, 28-30 YEARS OLD.
...
HIGH CHOLESTEROL.
SNFF
PURIFIERS.
MATTHEW RISMAN, WHITE MALE, 34-36, PREVIOUSLY AN ASSASSIN-FOR-HIRE, ACCORDING TO O*N*E AND S.H.I.E.L.D. FILES.
HE WAS PRESENT AT THE INSTITUTE DURING THE PURIFIER ATTACK LAST YEAR AND PERSONALLY RESPONSIBLE FOR THE DEATHS OF 42 XAVIER INSTITUTE STUDENTS KILLED IN A SINGLE ROCKET STRIKE.

RISMAN HAD AN INSIDE MAN, AGENT JEREMY LATCHAM. WHITE MALE, NO FAMILY, AGE 32. HIS FILE IS CLEAN. RELIGIOUS PREFERENCE: CHRISTIAN. CROSS-REFERENCE...
HIS MINISTRY IS ONE OF STRYKER'S.
A COMPUTER VIRUS WAS INTRODUCED INTO THE SYSTEM. ALL DATA REGARDING THE STOLEN OBJECT IS GONE. SUGGEST TRACKING AGENT JEREMY LATCHAM...WAIT.
WELL DONE, BROTHER JEREMY. THE LORD AWAITS YOU WITH OPEN ARMS.
THANK YOU, FATHER.
I CANNOT TRACK AGENT LATCHAM. HE PERFORMED SELF-TERMINATION TO PROTECT MISSION INTELLIGENCE...
...AND GIVEN THE CURRENT DATA, I CANNOT IDENTIFY THE STOLEN ITEM...
BUT I HAVE RISMAN'S SCENT.
I CAN TRACK HIM. WHAT IS MY MISSION?

STAY WITH HIM, REPORT BACK ONCE YOU HAVE HIS LOCATION.
GOOD WORK, LAURA.
CHOK!!
UHN!!
LAURA IS MY RESPONSIBILITY. YOU SHOULD HAVE COME TO ME FIRST, SUMMERS.
IS THIS WHO YOU ARE NOW? YOU JUST USE HER LIKE THIS? YOU SET UP WARPATH TO GO DOWN LIKE HIS BROTHER? YOU PULL IN RAHNE SINCLAIR TO THIS WORLD?
IF YOU WANT RISMAN DEAD, YOU COME TO ME. BUT I'LL DO IT ALONE.
THIS TEAM IS HAPPENING, LOGAN. YOU THINK I DON'T KNOW THE LINE I'M CROSSING? I DO. THIS ISN'T X-MEN WORK.
THIS IS X-FORCE. NO ONE CAN KNOW.

I'M NOT ASKING FOR YOUR PERMISSION, LOGAN. YOU KNOW IT'S WHAT HAS TO BE DONE.
AND FOR THE RECORD... RAHNE CAME TO ME.
LOGAN...
NOT IN A MILLION YEARS, DARLIN'. TRUST ME... YOU DON'T WANT THIS.
WHATEVER PERSONAL BAGGAGE YOU'VE GOT, JUST LOSE IT. FORGET ABOUT THIS.
I CAN'T.
I HAVE TO KNOW.
GRRRR...

OUTSIDE FARGO, NORTH DAKOTA. A CHURCH OF THE REVEREND WILLIAM STRYKER.
REVEREND STRYKER WAS GIVEN A GIFT FROM THE LORD...
A HOLY MESSENGER CALLED NIMROD THAT WOULD TELL THE FAITHFUL OF THE FUTURE AND LIGHT OUR WAY TO THE PATH OF REDEMPTION.
THE REVEREND WAS SHOWN MANY VISIONS, AND THE FUTURE WAS CHANGING BEFORE HIS VERY EYES. HE WAS TURNING THE TIDE AGAINST DARKNESS...HE WAS RETURNING EDEN TO HUMANITY AND DRIVING BACK SATAN'S MUTANTS...
...AND THEN HE WAS TAKEN FROM US.
WHEN WE STRUCK OUT AGAINST THE CHILDREN OF SATAN THEY CUT OUR BELOVED FATHER DOWN, FILLING HIM WITH BLACK CANCEROUS TUMORS.
AND FOR THOSE OF US THAT SURVIVED THE BATTLE, WE RETURNED TO FIND OUR CHURCH DESTROYED, OUR BROTHERS DEAD AND THE LORD'S MESSENGER STOLEN.
WE EVENTUALLY RECLAIMED NIMROD FROM THE WRECKAGE OF A MUTANT STRONGHOLD IN TEXAS BUT WE DIDN'T FIND HIM IN TIME...
HIS CONNECTION TO THE FUTURE WAS SEVERED AND WE ARE UNABLE TO RESTORE HIS POWER...
BUT YOU, BROTHER ELI, HAVE GIVEN US NEW HOPE.

FOOTFALL, POINT TWO-SEVEN KILOMETERS SOUTH SOUTHWEST. TWO MEN.
HE'S HERE, WITH JAMES PROUDSTAR.
THE ITEM IS HERE, AS IS RISMAN. THERE ARE SEVEN GUARDS CONCEALED AROUND THE EXTERIOR OF THE BUILDING.
THE LAYOUT IS SIMILAR TO THE WASHINGTON D.C. LOCATION, WITH THE ENTRANCE TO THE SUB-LEVELS THE MOST HEAVILY GUARDED.
ALL SEVEN GUARDS WILL HAVE TO BE KILLED TO GAIN ENTRY WITHOUT TRIGGERING ALARMS. WE'LL HAVE SIX MINUTES BEFORE RADIO SILENCE WILL BE QUESTIONED.

WELL "HELLO" TO YOU, TOO.

OKAY...I DON'T KNOW WHAT BAG OF GOODS CYCLOPS SOLD YOU, BUT BOTH OF YOU NEED TO WALK AWAY FROM THIS, RIGHT NOW.
YOU DO THIS, YOU'RE NOT X-MEN ANYMORE. YOU MAY BE ON THE TEAM, YOU MAY BE STANDING NEXT TO BEAST AND ANGEL AND ICEMAN, BUT YOU WON'T BE THE SAME AS THEM.
NOT AFTER THIS.
LAURA, YOU KEEP HEADING DOWN THIS PATH, AND ANY SHOT YOU HAD AT BEING HUMAN SLIPS FURTHER AWAY.
YOU DO THIS, AND YOU'RE X-23 AGAIN.
AND YOU, JIMMY...YOU'VE GOT NO PURPOSE IN LIFE, AND YOU DECIDE TO GO BACK TO REVENGE? IT DIDN'T WORK OUT FOR YOU BEFORE AND IT'S NOT GOING TO WORK OUT FOR YOU THIS TIME.
YOU'RE A BIG TOUGH MAN, I KNOW. BUT YOU DO THIS, AND YOU'RE SOMETHING ELSE. YOU'RE JUST A KILLER.
THIS IS YOUR LAST CHANCE TO MAKE THE RIGHT CHOICE.
WALK. AWAY.
FINE.
YOUR LIVES.

"ELI, YOU ARE THE FIRST BROTHER TO SEEK US OUT. ALL OF THE OTHERS THAT STAND AROUND US WERE BROUGHT IN BY REVEREND STRYKER HIMSELF. HE FOUND EACH ONE OF US AND PUT US ON THE ROAD TO SALVATION...
"YOU FOUND US AND LED US DIRECTLY TO THE DEVICE WE BELIEVE WILL RESTORE NIMROD.
"NIMROD WAS FROM THE FUTURE, NOT OUR OWN BUT ONE SIMILAR TO OURS. IN HIS TIMELINE, MUTANTS WERE ALL BUT EXTINCT...THE MACHINES OF MAN HAD TAKEN THE WORLD BACK FROM THEM.
"BUT WHEN NIMROD FOUND OUR REVEREND, HE CONNECTED TO OUR TIMELINE AND COULD SHOW US HOW OUR ACTIONS CHANGED OUR OWN FUTURE.
"NIMROD'S OBITUARIES CONTAINED DEATHS YET TO HAPPEN AND WE USED THEM TO SAVE THE LIVES OF THOSE THAT SHOULD HAVE BEEN LOST. AND THOSE THAT WERE SAVED, LIKE MYSELF, JOINED IN THE FIGHT AGAINST SATAN.
"BUT NIMROD IS NOT JUST A MESSENGER FROM THE FUTURE. HE IS A WARRIOR DESIGNED SOLELY TO SLAY DEMONS...TO SLAY MUTANTS. HE, ABOVE ALL OTHERS, CAN TURN THE TIDE AGAINST THE MUTANT THREAT...HE DID IT IN HIS TIME, HE CAN DO IT IN OURS."
UNTIL YOU FOUND US, WE BELIEVED THIS WAS THE ONLY OCCASION WHEN NIMROD CAME TO OUR PAST. BUT NOW WE SEE THAT HE HAD BEEN HERE BEFORE...THAT WHILE LEAPING BACK IN TIME, THIS WAS BUT HIS FIRST STOP...
HE CONTINUED TO MOVE FURTHER BACK IN OUR TIME AND ARRIVED ON A SECOND OCCASION...MANY YEARS AGO.
THERE AGAIN, HE FOUGHT AGAINST MUTANTS AND EVENTUALLY MERGED WITH ANOTHER MACHINE CALLED MASTER MOLD...HE BECAME SOMETHING EVEN GREATER THAN THE BEING WE SEE BEFORE US...

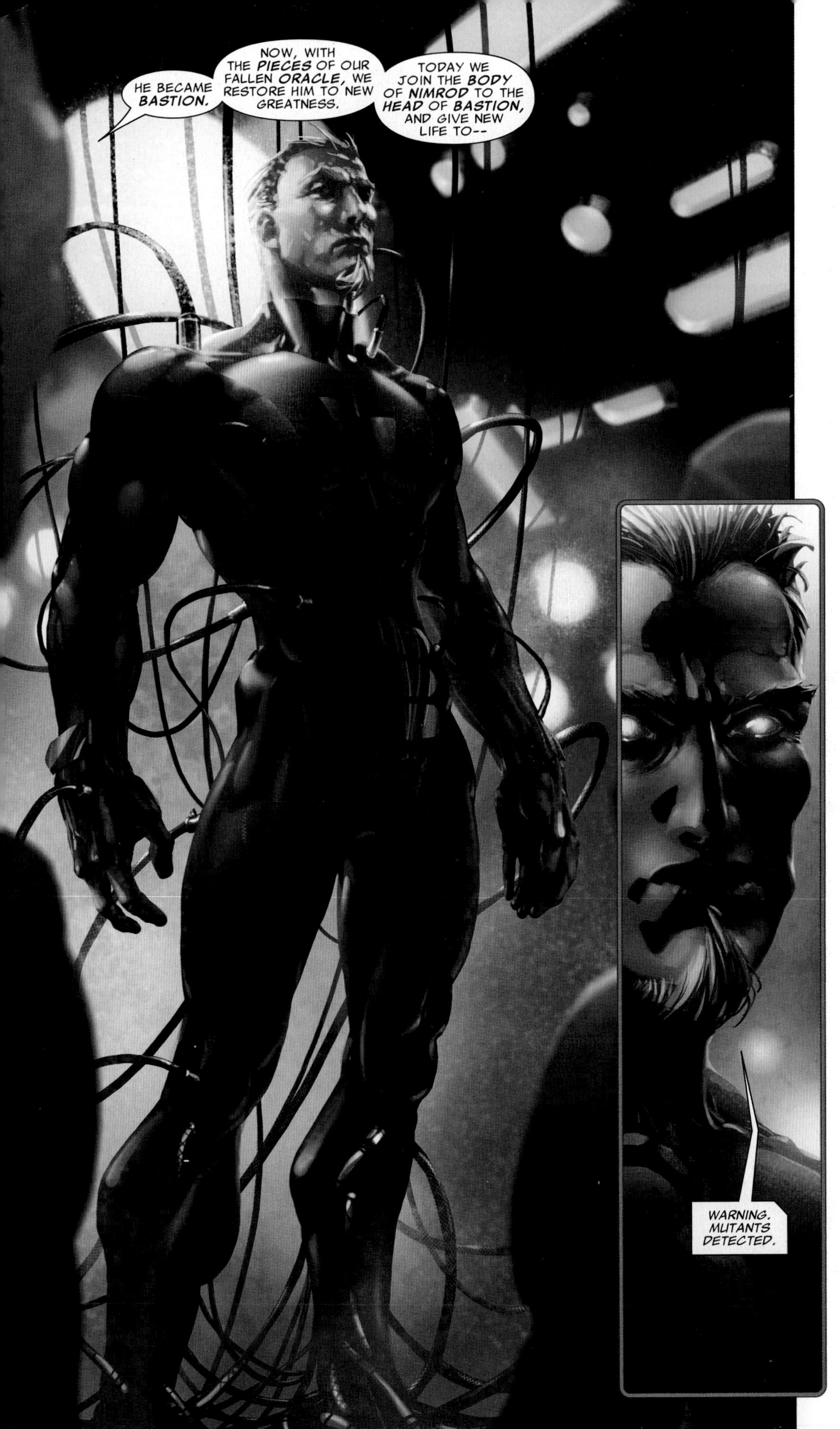
HE BECAME BASTION.
NOW, WITH THE PIECES OF OUR FALLEN ORACLE, WE RESTORE HIM TO NEW GREATNESS.
TODAY WE JOIN THE BODY OF NIMROD TO THE HEAD OF BASTION, AND GIVE NEW LIFE TO--
WARNING. MUTANTS DETECTED.

RRRAAA!!
AIIEEE!!
AAARRGH!!
AAAAHHH!
BUDDABUDDABUDDA!
THUNK!!
X, BEHIND YOU!!
THOK!!

DIE, MUTANT SC--

CHUNK!

--*

HE WAS GOING TO KILL YOU. SO, I- I KILLED HIM.

YES, YOU DID.

RISMAN.

HE'S NOT ALONE. HE'S GOT--

STAND DOWN...
...OR THE MUTANT *DIES.*

RAHNE?!
SHE DIES, YOU FOLLOW HER ONE SECOND LATER, RISMAN.
HE'S LYING... HE DOESN'T *WANT* TO KILL HER.
X, DON'T--
AAAIIEE!!
SLIK!
AAARRGHH!
I DON'T *BLUFF*, MUTANT.
BLAM!!

-Crain-

OUTSIDE FARGO, NORTH DAKOTA. THE CHURCH OF THE REVEREND WILLIAM STRYKER. NOW.
THE PURIFIERS ATTACK US INSIDE OUR OWN BASE AND WHEN WE CATCH UP TO THEM 76 HOURS LATER, THIS IS WHAT WE FIND...

I WANT TO KNOW WHY, AND I WANT TO KNOW WHO'S RESPONSIBLE.
THE HEAT FROM THE FIRE WAS SO INTENSE IT LIQUEFIED THE MORTAR IN THE WALLS. YOU DON'T GET TEMPERATURES LIKE THIS UNDER NORMAL FIRE CONDITIONS...
WHATEVER WAS USED HERE WAS GOVERNMENT GRADE OR BETTER.
SPREAD OUT. GET ME ANSWERS.

MORALES TO HILL. IF RISMAN'S HERE, WE MAY NOT BE ABLE TO POSITIVELY I.D. HIM. MOST OF THE BODIES WE'VE FOUND HAVE BEEN CREMATED BY THE FIRE.
KEEP ME INFORMED...BUT JUST ME. DIRECTOR STARK WANTS THIS KEPT DARK UNTIL WE'VE IDENTIFIED ANY OTHER PURIFIER OPERATIVES PLANTED INSIDE S.H.I.E.L.D.
MARIA HILL
UNDERSTOOD.
AGENT MORALES! WE'VE GOT MORE BODIES UNDERGROUND. A LOT MORE.
AND THEY DIDN'T DIE FROM THE FIRE.

ELEVEN HOURS AGO.

RAHNE!!

AFTER ALL THE MUTANTS I'VE TAKEN FROM YOUR INSTITUTE, DID YOU REALLY THINK I WOULDN'T KILL ONE MORE?

THIS IS *MATTHEW RISMAN.*

HE'S A DEAD MAN.

CYCLOPS ORDERED X-FORCE TO TAKE DOWN THE PURIFIERS, AND RAHNE WANTED IN. I SAID NO.
GNNN... NN...
SO SHE CAME BY HERSELF, AHEAD OF US, AND GOT CAPTURED.
NOW SHE'S GOT A BULLET IN HER KNEE. BEST-CASE SCENARIO IS SHE GETS OUT OF THIS WITH A LIMP.
WORST-CASE IS SHE DOESN'T GET OUT.
THEY DRUGGED HER.
HEROIN.
FORTUNATELY FOR YOUR FRIEND, I AM A MAN OF GOD AND DECIDED TO SHOW HER MERCY NOT DESERVING OF YOUR KIND...
BUT I AM ONLY HUMAN, AND HAVE MY LIMITS.
SO, SURRENDER NOW...
OR SHE BEGINS HER ETERNAL SUFFERING IN HELL TONIGHT.

DO WHAT HE SAYS, X.
HE'S LYING.
WE'RE NOT RISKING RAHNE'S LIFE ON A HUNCH... NOW, **STAND DOWN.**
YOU'RE **DEAD**, DO YOU HEAR ME, RISMAN? ALL OF YOU ARE--
WHUMP
UHH!!
ON YOUR KNEES, DEMON!
YOU HAVE THE EYES OF A **KILLER**, GIRL...NOT LIKE WOLVERINE. NO, HE'S JUST AN ANIMAL. BUT YOU...YOU WERE **BRED** FOR MURDER.
AND RIGHT NOW YOU'RE THINKING OF ELEVEN DIFFERENT WAYS TO KILL ME, AREN'T YOU?
NO... **TWENTY-SEVEN.**
HEH. I BELIEVE YOU.
HE WILL NOT KILL HER.
STAND THE $%@# DOWN, X!
NOW!!
THIS IS A MISTAKE.
BIND THEM ALL.

CRAP LIKE THIS IS WHY I'M NO LEADER.
THUD!
HNN!
ANY OTHER TIME, THIS GUY WOULD HAVE LOST HIS HAND FOR THAT.
ANY OTHER TIME, I'D HAVE GIVEN IN TO THE BEAST INSIDE ME AND RISMAN'S INTESTINES WOULD BE DECORATING THIS PLACE.
BUT NOW I'M RESPONSIBLE FOR--
FATHER MATTHEW? THE GIRL...
...SHE'S HOLDING SOMETHING.
SHE'S GOT A--
X, DON'T!!!
CLICK
AW, $#%@.

SHOOOOM!
AAAAHHH--
THIS IS GONNA HURT.
HURK!
OH, SH--
MISSION CONTINGENCY ACTIVATED.
TARGET RISMAN IS ALIVE AND ON THE MOVE.
PURSUING.

HK! HURK!!
HURTS A HELL OF A LOT MORE COMING OUT.
LAURA'S AFTER RISMAN. I HAVE TO GET TO JIMMY.
WARPATH!! YOU BETTER BE ALIVE, DAMMIT!!
WHERE'S RAHNE?
RISMAN MADE OFF WITH HER. YOU OKAY?
YEAH, PURIFIERS TOOK THE BRUNT.
WELL, AT LEAST THEY'RE GOOD FOR SOMETHING.
COME ON, WE NEED TO GET TO LAURA BEFORE SHE GETS RAHNE KILLED.

THE GIRL IS FOLLOWING ME.
KILL HER.
MULTIPLE TARGETS.
BLAM!
BLAM!
BLAM!
TARGETS ELIMINATED. STAY ON RISMAN.
TAKE OFF! NOW!!
SIR, GET DOWN!
BLAM! BLAM! BLAM!
GUH!!
CLICK CLICK CLICK
WEAPON IS OUT OF AMMUNITION. TARGET IS ESCAPING...
COLLECTING VISUAL DATA. TWO KNOWN OCCUPANTS. TWO UNKNOWN.
CANNOT MAKE VISUAL ON THE LAST OCCUPANT.
RAHNE! RAHNE!!
I FAILED.
I'M GONNA KILL SUMMERS.

ANGEL'S AERIE, THE COLORADO ROCKY MOUNTAINS. NOW.
WHAT THE @#$% WAS THAT?!
DID YOU FORGET TO MENTION THAT YOU WIRED THE WHOLE DAMN PLACE TO BLOW?
YOU AND I, WE CAN BE BURNED, BLOWN UP, AND TAKE A THOUSAND ROUNDS IN THE CHEST--BUT WARPATH AND WOLFSBANE CAN'T!
THEY SURVIVED.
WHAT IS THE MATTER WITH YOU, LAURA?! RISMAN'S STILL GOT RAHNE AND HE'S GOING TO KILL HER!
SAVING WOLFSBANE WAS NOT MY MISSION.
WHAT THE HELL IS THAT SUPPOSED TO MEAN?!
SHE MEANS EXACTLY WHAT SHE SAID. HER MISSION WAS TO ELIMINATE MATTHEW RISMAN, NOT PERFORM A SEARCH AND RESCUE.

THIS SITUATION WITH RAHNE IS YOUR DOING, LOGAN. NOT HERS.
IS THAT SO?
DAMN RIGHT IT IS. IF YOU'D LET RAHNE EXPLAIN WHAT SHE WAS AFTER, YOU'D HAVE KNOWN HOW DETERMINED SHE WAS TO GET INSIDE.
SO IF ANYTHING HAPPENS TO HER NOW, IT'S ON YOU.
LOOK, BUB--
AW, HELL.
WARREN.
PRETTY SNEAKY, COMING IN DOWNWIND.
WHEN MY HOME IS BEING USED FOR CLANDESTINE MEETINGS, YEAH. I CAN DO SNEAKY.
NOW... IF ANYTHING HAPPENS TO WHO?
DON'T LOOK AT ME--ASK XAVIER JUNIOR HERE.
HE'S THE ONE CALLIN' THE SHOTS.
WARREN...IT'S COMPLICATED.
SOMEONE'S LIFE IS IN DANGER, SCOTT. IT DOESN'T GET ANY LESS COMPLICATED THAN THAT.
LOOK, I ASKED YOU BEFORE TO STAY OUT OF THIS, AND I NEED YOU TO KEEP STAYING OUT OF IT, NOW.
LIVES ARE ON THE LINE AND YOU WON'T TELL ME WHOSE LIFE--OR WHAT'S GOING ON?
IT'S RAHNE. SHE'S BEEN CAPTURED BY THE PURIFIERS.

DAMMIT, WARPATH...

WHAT ARE WE WAITING FOR?

WE HAVE TO TELL THE OTHERS! WE HAVE TO FIND HER!

NO WE DON'T.

LOOK, WE KNOW THE PURIFIERS *ONLY* CARE ABOUT *KILLING MUTANTS...* CHILDREN, BABIES, EVEN FORMER MUTANTS...

BUT THEY'VE *CAPTURED* WOLFSBANE AND KEPT HER *ALIVE* TO THIS POINT, SO RIGHT NOW WE'RE DEALING WITH SOMETHING *ELSE* ENTIRELY.

FOR WHATEVER REASON, RAHNE'S SAFE FOR NOW AND WE'LL GET HER BACK.

BUT IF WE GET THE X-MEN INVOLVED, WE'RE PUTTING HER AT EVEN MORE RISK AND GUARANTEEING SOMEONE ON OUR SIDE *WILL* GET KILLED.

WHY WOULD SHE *DO* THIS? WHY GO AFTER THEM BY HERSELF?

SHE WANTED REVENGE.

NO! YOU DON'T KNOW RAHNE, SHE'D NEVER WANT THAT.

WHAT DO YOU KNOW ABOUT *REVEREND CRAIG?*

HE'S THE *SADISTIC BASTARD* WHO RAISED RAHNE. HE *BEAT* RELIGION INTO HER AND FORCED HER TO BELIEVE SHE WAS *EVIL* BECAUSE SHE WAS BORN A *MUTANT.*

THAT'S RIGHT. AND WOLFSBANE JUST FOUND OUT THAT HE'S JOINED THE PURIFIERS.

"WHEN RAHNE AND I FIRST MET, SHE KNEW ALL ABOUT MY BROTHER AND WE USED TO SWAP STORIES...
"I TOLD HER ABOUT JOHNNY AND SHE USED TO TALK ABOUT CRAIG..."
HNNN...

"RAHNE TOLD ME THAT REVEREND CRAIG BELIEVED THAT SHE WAS A TEST FROM GOD."
WHAT... WHERE AM I?
"THAT SHE WAS A LIVING SIN, SENT TO HIM FOR CLEANSING."

WHAT IS--
"BUT SHE HAD TO FIND OUT THE TRUTH ABOUT HIM ON HER OWN."
ARE YE AWAKE NOW, SINNER?
"CRAIG WASN'T JUST THE MAN WHO RAISED HER...

"HE WAS ALSO HER..."
F-FATHER?

WHAT ARE YOU DOING HERE? WHAT ARE YOU DOING WITH THE PURIFIERS?
NO. YE ARE NOT MY FLESH AND BLOOD.
SATAN'S DAUGHTER YE ARE, DEMON. AND YE WILL ADDRESS ME AS "REVEREND."
FROM THE SECOND I RECOGNIZED YE FOR WHAT YE WERE, I KNEW THAT SATAN'S SPAWN WALKED GOD'S EARTH.
BUT I THOUGHT I WAS ALONE IN FIGHTING YE.
NOW I'VE LEARNED WHY I WAS MADE TO SUFFER YOUR EXISTENCE.
BUT NO MORE.
NO...STOP! WHAT ARE YOU DOING?
NO... UHHH... WHAT DID YOU...
I AM TO BE YOUR INQUISITOR.
I WILL LISTEN TO YOUR SINS, AND YE WILL MAKE AMENDS TO THE LORD FOR POISONING EDEN WITH YOUR WICKEDNESS.
"YOU SEEM CONCERNED, MATTHEW. IS IT THE REVEREND CRAIG? HE DOES SEEMS A BIT...UNSTABLE."
"YOU'RE VERY PERCEPTIVE, BROTHER ELI. BUT NO, IT'S NOT CRAIG. HE'LL DO WHAT WE REQUIRE OF HIM.
"IT'S BASTION."

HE WON'T MEET WITH ME, HE WON'T EVEN SPEAK TO ME. HE'S EFFECTIVELY TAKEN OVER THE PURIFIERS, AND ISN'T INFORMING ME OF HIS PLANS.
MATTHEW RISMAN...
...WHAT DO YOU THINK YOU ARE DOING?
BASTION...REVEREND STRYKER LEFT SPECIFIC INSTRUCTIONS FOR RAHNE SINCLAIR. SHE WAS CHOSEN TO--
KILL THE MUTANT.
WHAT? I-I CAN'T...PLEASE LET ME EXPLAIN-- THERE IS A PLAN--
NO. WE HAVE ANALYZED YOUR "PLAN."
IT HAS A 99.74 PERCENT PROBABILITY OF FAILURE.
ITS FAILURE HAS ALREADY BEGUN...

OMAHA, NEBRASKA.
"THE X-MEN HAVE SENT THEIR TRACKERS AND KILLERS AFTER YOU, MATHEW RISMAN.
"WOLVERINE. WARPATH. X-23.
"EVEN AS WE SPEAK, THEY ARE RAIDING PURIFIER BASES.
WICHITA, KANSAS.
TULSA, OKLAHOMA.
"THEY WILL TORTURE AND KILL EVERY PURIFIER THEY FIND, ALL TO RECOVER THEIR TEAMMATE.
"AND EVENTUALLY, MATTHEW RISMAN... THEY WILL KILL YOU."

HE'S NOT GOING TO REALLY DO IT, IS HE?
YES, HE IS.
THIS IS GONNA HURT A LITTLE.
NOT... AFRAID OF YOU... MUTANT...
I WASN'T TALKING ABOUT YOU, BUB. YOU'RE NOT GOING TO FEEL A THING.
NNN! THE CLAW... IT GETS SO HOT THAT WHEN I SLICE OFF YOUR EAR, YOUR NERVOUS SYSTEM WILL JUST... SHUT DOWN.
YOUR HANDS, YOUR NOSE, AN EYE... THE WOUNDS WILL CAUTERIZE, AND I'LL KEEP YOU ALIVE UNTIL YOU GIVE ME WHAT I NEED...
'COURSE, GETTING A DATE AFTER THIS IS GOING TO BE A LITTLE ROUGH.
PAF!
I'LL DO WHATEVER IT TAKES TO GET RAHNE BACK... BUT YOU AND LOGAN... HOW CAN YOU BOTH BE SO INDIFFERENT TO ALL THIS BLOOD?
I DO NOT UNDERSTAND YOUR QUESTION.
NEVER MIND.
I GOT A LOCATION.

REVEREND STRYKER ENTRUSTED ME WITH TWO THINGS, SHOULD HE EVER BE KILLED...TO PROTECT THE ORACLE AND TO CREATE THE CHOIR.
AND THAT'S WHAT I INTEND TO DO.
WILLIAM STRYKER WAS A FLAWED MAN.
THAT "FLAWED MAN" ENGINEERED YOUR RESURRECTION. HOW CAN YOU--
ARE YOU DEFECTIVE, MATTHEW RISMAN?
WHAT?
ARE. YOU. DEFECTIVE?
MATTHEW...
NO. NO. I'M NOT DEFECTIVE.
I'LL LISTEN.
WE KNOW HOW TO ELIMINATE THE MUTANTS...BUT YOU DO NOT LISTEN TO US.
YET YOUR MISSION IS TO ELIMINATE THE MUTANTS. WHY WILL YOU NOT OBEY YOUR OWN MISSION?

WE CONCLUDED, AS DID THE FLAWED WILLIAM STRYKER, THAT THE **X-MEN** ARE THE GREATEST **MUTANT THREAT** IN THIS TIMELINE, OR ANY OTHER.

"SO THERE'S **NO WAY** TO STOP THEM?"

"INCORRECT. WE SAID THERE WAS NO **TERRESTRIAL** SOLUTION, MATTHEW RISMAN."

"THEN **WHERE?**"
WE'RE NEARING THE COORDINATES. SLOW DOWN.

BEFORE OUR **RESTORATION**, WE BECAME AWARE OF A CREATURE WITH THE ABILITY TO INFECT AND ABSORB **ORGANIC MATTER**, CONVERTING IT INTO **SUSTENANCE** OR **INFUSING** IT WITH ITS OWN **SENTIENCE**.
THE CREATURE WAS REVERTED TO A **NASCENT FORM**, AND LEFT ON THE BOTTOM OF THE OCEAN.
LEFT THERE BY THE **X-MEN**.

DEAR GOD...WHAT *IS* THIS?

"IT STAYED THERE FOR A VERY LONG TIME. GROWING. EVOLVING. REPLICATING."

"AND HOW WILL WE FIND IT?"

"IT WILL FIND *US*, MATTHEW RISMAN."

AHHHH!

"AND IF THIS 'CREATURE' IS SO DEADLY, WON'T IT JUST **KILL** WHOEVER COMES AFTER IT?"

TRANSMIT THE SIGNAL!!

"WE'VE GIVEN YOUR PURIFIERS A BEACON IT WILL RESPOND TO. A SINGLE WORD.

"WARLOCK."

"DOES YOUR CREATURE HAVE A NAME?"

"OH, YES."

MAGUS.

PRAGUE.

OPEN THE DOOR, MISTER PIERCE.

WHOEVER THESE PEOPLE ARE, THEY'VE CHASED ME ACROSS TWO CONTINENTS.

FINISH THIS. NOW!!

...ALMOST DONE...GOING AS FAST AS I--

MISTER PIERCE...

DIE!

AAAHH!

CHOOM! CHOOM! CHOOM!

YOU KNEW MY NAME, IDIOT, SO YOU SHOULD HAVE KNOWN NOT TO--

DONALD PIERCE...

...YOUR PRESENCE HAS BEEN REQUESTED.

GUATEMALA.

‹THE PRISONER HAS BEEN FOUND GUILTY OF THE PREMEDITATED MURDER OF A MINOR.›

‹PER THE LAWS OF THIS COUNTRY, SHE HAS BEEN SENTENCED TO DEATH. DOES THE ACCUSED HAVE ANY LAST WORDS?›

I REGRET THAT I WILL NOT SEE THE OTHER MUTANT DIE.

CHOOOM!

LEPER QUEEN. YOU HAVE BEEN SUMMONED.

BY WHO?

THE LORD.

MOUNT EVEREST.

THAT'S QUITE A DROP.
ANY READINGS?

YES, SISTER MARY. HE'S HERE.
THE ORACLE WILL BE PLEASED.
IT'S TIME TO COME HOME, MR. HODGE.

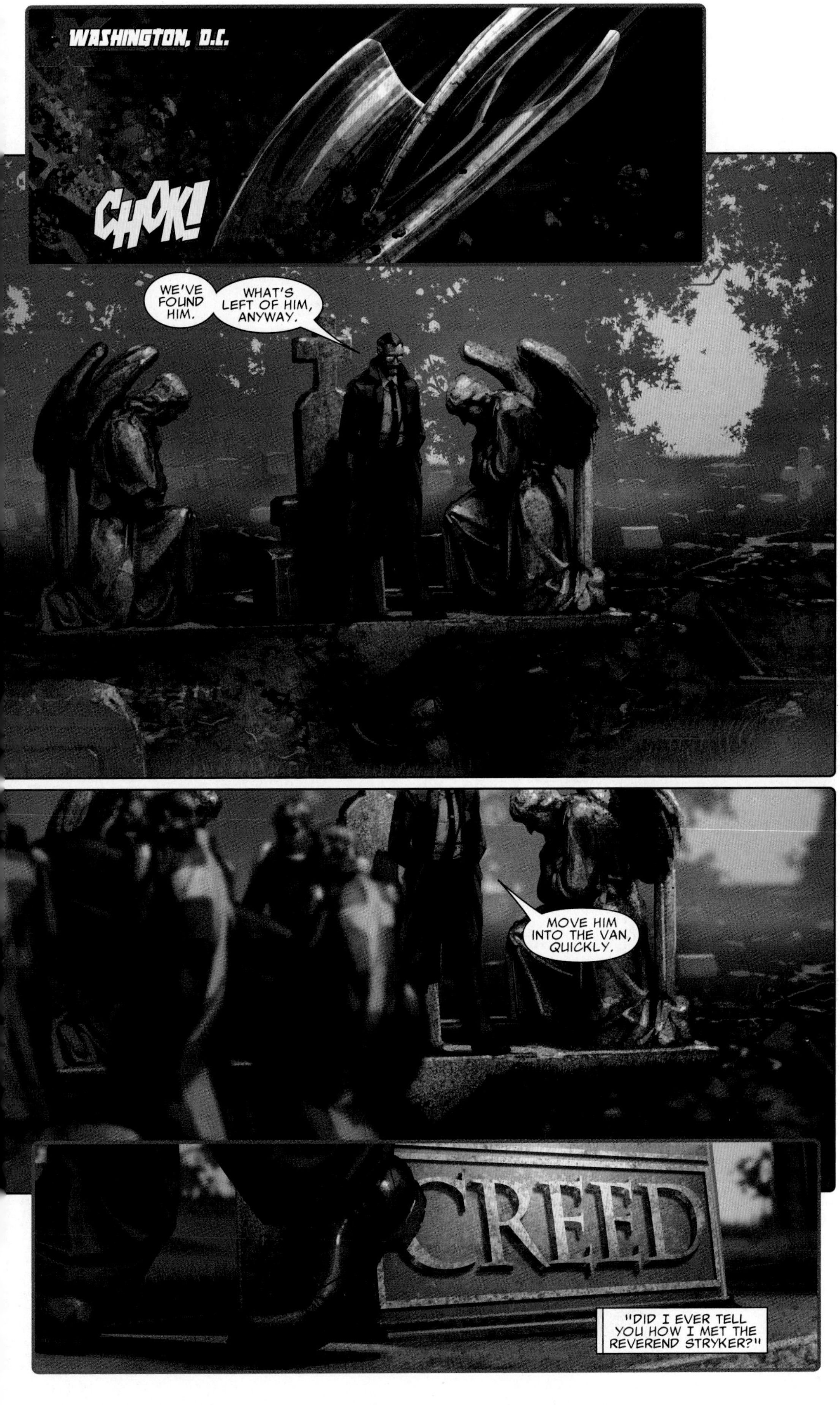

WASHINGTON, D.C.
CHOK!
WE'VE FOUND HIM.
WHAT'S LEFT OF HIM, ANYWAY.
MOVE HIM INTO THE VAN, QUICKLY.
CREED
"DID I EVER TELL YOU HOW I MET THE REVEREND STRYKER?"

I WAS IN THE MIDDLE OF A JOB WHEN HE FIRST CONTACTED ME.
HE SAID THE LORD HAD SENT HIM WITH AN URGENT MESSAGE AND THAT LIVES WOULD BE LOST IF I DID NOT HEED HIS WARNING.
AT FIRST I THOUGHT HE WAS CRAZY BUT IN THE END I LISTENED TO HIM...
...AND HE SAVED THE LIVES OF MY WIFE AND DAUGHTER.
SO YOU SEE, ELI, I OWE WILLIAM STRYKER *EVERYTHING.*
ONLY *HE* COULD HAVE SAVED MY FAMILY AND NOW ONLY *I* CAN INSURE HIS CRUSADE IS COMPLETED.
HIS PLANS AGAINST THE X-MEN ARE ALREADY IN MOTION AND I WILL NOT ALLOW THEM TO BE STOPPED.
BUT BASTION GAVE YOU SPECIFIC ORDERS...
AND THE ORACLE'S ORDERS *WILL* BE CARRIED OUT--BUT NOT AT THE COST OF WILLIAM STRYKER'S MISSION.
NOW TELL ME, REVEREND CRAIG. HOW DID IT FEEL TO DELIVER WOLFSBANE TO THE LORD?
RIGHTEOUS.

EAST OF MISSOULA, MONTANA.
MY NAME IS JAMES PROUDSTAR. I AM APACHE.
THESE ARE BLACKFOOT LANDS...
AND THESE LANDS ARE ABOUT TO GET A $#!^LOAD OF BLOOD SPILLED ON THEM.
LET'S DO THIS.
PURIFIER BLOOD.

THESE BASTARDS HAVE KILLED CHILDREN...THEY'VE KILLED BABIES, JUST BECAUSE THEY WERE MUTANTS.
AND THEY KILLED MY FRIEND CALIBAN...
I PROMISED HIM I'D MAKE THEM PAY.
BUT THE PURIFIERS HAVE MADE IT WORSE FOR THEMSELVES...
BECAUSE NOW THEY'VE TAKEN RAHNE, TOO.

WOLVERINE AND X-23 HAVE KILLED AND TORTURED THEIR WAY ACROSS THE MIDWEST, LOOKING FOR HER.
AND I'VE DONE THINGS IN THE LAST FEW DAYS I DIDN'T KNOW I WAS CAPABLE OF.
WHEN CYCLOPS CALLED US X-FORCE, I HELD MY TONGUE FOR ONCE.
X-FORCE WAS A TEAM OF KIDS TURNED INTO SOLDIERS...
THIS IS SOMETHING DIFFERENT.
BUT THIS, THE THREE OF US...
AND RIGHT THIS SECOND, I'M OKAY WITH THAT.

BECAUSE WHEN I FIND THE PURIFIERS...
WHEN I FIND THAT SON OF A BITCH WHO TOOK RAHNE, WHO PUT A *BULLET* IN HER...
IT WON'T BE WOLVERINE OR X-23 WHO TAKES HIM DOWN.
IT'LL BE ME.
AND I'M GOING TO KILL MATTHEW RISMAN WITH MY BARE--

RAHNE!!

CHICAGO.
NEGATIVE MUTANT PRESENCE.
THE GIRL ISN'T ON BOARD.
NO, ORACLE. ONLY THE THREE.
FATHER...
BASTION.
I TRUST THIS PURIFIER BASE HAS MET YOUR NEEDS.
IS THE MUTANT DEAD?

MONTANA.
RAHNE!!
NO, PLEASE GOD, NOT AGAIN...
THOSE WERE YOUR ORDERS.
DID. YOU. KILL HER?!
RAHNE?
YES.
SHE'S STILL ALIVE! WE HAVE TO GET HER HELP! MOVE!
HNNN...

WHERE ARE YOU TAKING US?
INCORRECT. THE QUESTION IS, WHERE ARE WE TAKING YOU? THE OUTSIDER IS NOT COMING WITH US.
EXCUSE ME?
"ELI BARD"...
REAL NAME: UNKNOWN... FORMER ALIASES: UNKNOWN... IDENTITY: UNKNOWN... OCCUPATION: UNKNOWN... LEGAL STATUS: UNKNOWN... PLACE OF BIRTH: UNKNOWN...
MARITAL STATUS: UNKNOWN... BASE OF OPERATIONS: UNKNOWN... GROUP AFFILIATION: UNKNOWN... FIRST APPEARANCE: UNKNOWN...
YOU CALL YOURSELF "ELI BARD" BUT WE HAVE NO RECORD OF YOU, PRESENT OR FUTURE.
WE DO NOT KNOW YOU, AND WE DO NOT TRUST YOU.

WITH ALL DUE RESPECT, BASTION, BUT IF NOT FOR BROTHER ELI, YOU WOULDN'T BE HERE.
HE'S THE ONE THAT LED US TO YOU.
HURK!!
IRRELEVANT.
MATTHEW...
YOU SAID YOU DON'T KNOW ANYTHING ABOUT HIM, SO WHY KILL HIM NOW?
LET ME FIND OUT WHO HE IS, AND IF HE'S AGAINST US...I'LL BE THE ONE TO KILL HIM.
ACCEPTABLE.
YOU'RE A GOOD MAN, ELI...I'LL GET YOU OUT OF THIS.
I PROMISE.

WHAT IN HEAVEN'S NAME...
THIS HAS NOTHING TO DO WITH HEAVEN, MATTHEW RISMAN.
THIS IS THE WORK OF MAN.
YOU DON'T KNOW WHO YOU'RE DEALING WITH! I HAVE FRIENDS IN POWERFUL PLACES, DO YOU HEAR ME?!
WE KNOW ALL ABOUT YOUR FRIENDS, DONALD PIERCE. WHY DO YOU THINK YOU ARE HERE?
BASTION!!
IS THIS THE APOCALYPSE AGAIN?
WILL IT HURT?
WHO ARE THESE PEOPLE? BASTION, WHAT ARE YOU--
DEAR GOD.

WE FORGET THAT SEEING A TECHNO-ORGANIC CREATURE FOR THE FIRST TIME CAN BE...UNSETTLING.
THIS IS MAGUS. OR, PERHAPS MORE ACCURATELY, A MINDLESS OFFSPRING OF MAGUS.
PERHAPS BETTER THIS CREATURE DOES NOT POSSESS ITS FATHER'S INTELLECT. IT WILL MAKE REWRITING ITS PROGRAMMING THAT MUCH EASIER.
SKEEEEEE!!

NOW WE/ SELF AM/ARE IN CONTROL.
NOW SELF/ WE ARE/ AM TECHNARCHY/ NOT TECHNARCHY.
CHOK!
CHOK!
YEARRRGHH!!
AAAIIEEEEE!!!

COLORADO.

ANGEL'S AERIE.

WHAT THE--?

WARPATH!?

JAMES! WHAT HAPPENED? IS SHE OKAY?

DOES SHE *LOOK* OKAY, WORTHINGTON?!

SHE'S SEIZING!

HK! HKK!!

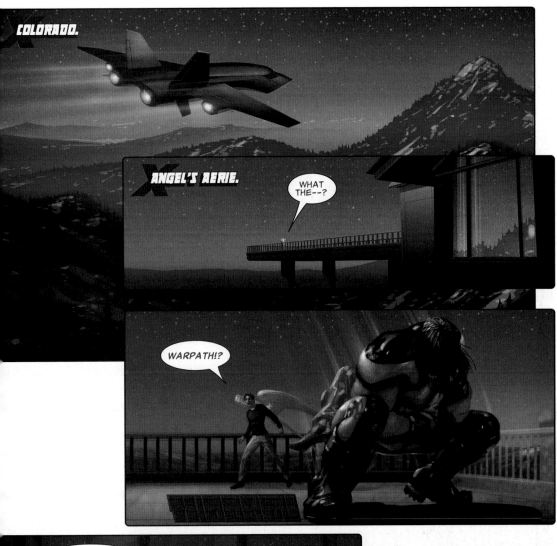

COME ON, RAHNEY, YOU CAN DO THIS... JUST HOLD ON...
NNN!!
WHAT HAPPENED?
THE PURIFIERS INJECTED HER WITH AN OVERDOSE OF HEROIN...
BUT THEY SHOULD HAVE KNOWN IT WASN'T A LETHAL AMOUNT.
LET ME HELP, LOGAN.
YOU WANNA HELP?
THEN GO FIND ELIXIR RIGHT FREAKING NOW!

BASTION... WHAT YOU'VE DONE...
WE EXPLAINED THAT THERE WAS NO EXISTING TERRESTRIAL FORCE THAT COULD GUARANTEE THE TOTAL ELIMINATION OF THE X-MEN...
YES...BUT WHAT YOU'VE DONE...IT'S UNHOLY. WE NEVER SHOULD HAVE--
WE HAVE CREATED A TERRESTRIAL SOLUTION TO THE X-MEN AND THE GLOBAL MUTANT THREAT.
THE FIRST STAGE IS COMPLETE.
FROM HERE, WE EXPAND.
TAKE YOUR PLACE, MATTHEW RISMAN.
THIS IS THE FUTURE OF HUMANITY.

THIS IS THE END OF MUTANTKIND.
GRAYDON CREED
FOUNDER OF FRIENDS OF HUMANITY
MUTANTS KILLED: 147
DONALD PIERCE
LEADER OF THE REAVERS
MUTANTS KILLED: 348
STEPHEN LANG
HEAD OF PROJECT: ARMAGEDDON
MUTANTS KILLED: 29

EVEREND WILLIAM STRYKER
ARCHBISHOP OF THE PURIFIERS
MUTANTS KILLED: 414
THE LEPER QUEEN
LEADER OF THE SAPIEN LEAGUE
MUTANTS KILLED: 221
CAMERON HODGE
FOUNDER OF THE RIGHT
MUTANTS KILLED: 178
BOLIVAR TRASK
INVENTOR OF THE SENTINELS
MUTANTS KILLED: 16,527,678

MY DESIGNATION IS "X-23."
I WAS THE 23RD EMBRYO CREATED BY THE FACILITY IN A PROJECT DESIGNED TO CLONE THE MUTANT CALLED WEAPON X.
HRRNNNN!!!...
THE FACILITY CONDITIONED ME FROM BIRTH TO BE THE PERFECT LIVING WEAPON AND TRAINED ME IN THE SKILLS NEEDED TO TRACK AND KILL ANY TARGET, ANYWHERE.
MY GOD...
GIVE ME GOOD NEWS, GOLDEN BOY.
AT THIRTEEN, I KILLED MY CREATORS...INCLUDING MY MOTHER, DR. SARAH KINNEY.
NOW I TAKE ORDERS FROM CYCLOPS.
HER LEG IS HEALED...
MY FIRST MISSION WAS TO FIND AND KILL THE PURIFIER MATTHEW RISMAN, BUT BEFORE I COULD COMPLETE MY ASSIGNMENT, RAHNE SINCLAIR WAS CAPTURED.
SHE WAS HELD FOR DAYS, BUT THEN RELEASED AFTER RECEIVING A NEAR-LETHAL DOSE OF HEROIN.
...AND I'M PURGING THE DRUGS FROM HER SYSTEM NOW.
HER SURVIVAL IS INCONSISTENT WITH THE PURIFIERS' PREVIOUS ACTIONS. I DO NOT BELIEVE THEY INTENDED TO KILL HER WITH THE OVERDOSE.
I TRIED TO SEPARATE THE HEROIN FROM HER BLOOD CELLS AND EVEN THOUGH I COULDN'T GET ALL OF IT...
SHE'LL BE OKAY... PHYSICALLY.
IT IS CLEAR THAT THE PURIFIERS' OBJECTIVES HAVE CHANGED, BUT THE EMOTIONAL CONNECTION THE OTHERS SHARE WITH SINCLAIR PREVENTS THEM FROM LISTENING TO ME.
NOW OUR MISSION IS AT RISK.
I'LL GO TELL LOGAN.
NO... I'LL DO IT.

COLORADO.
I HAVE STUDIED WEAPON X ALL OF MY LIFE. BUT HE IS NOT LIKE THE FERAL MUTANT I WAS TRAINED TO KILL...
HE IS VERY EMOTIONAL FOR A WEAPON.
RAHNE WAS ONE OF THE FIRST KIDS THAT CHUCK BROUGHT INTO THE SCHOOL AFTER I GOT THERE.
CHUCK...PROFESSOR CHARLES XAVIER. STATUS, UNKNOWN.
SHE WAS ONE OF THE NEW MUTANTS... AND I HELPED TRAIN HER.
THEN SHE SHOULD HAVE KNOWN BETTER.
HIS ENTIRE SCENT CHANGES IN AN INSTANT. I HAVE ANGERED HIM.
HHN.
SHUT UP AND LISTEN!

RAHNE SINCLAIR HAS TWO THINGS WE'LL NEVER GET BACK...**HOPE** AND **INNOCENCE.**

SHE'S **WHO** WE **SAVE**--SHE'S **WHY** WE RISK OUR LIVES.

SHE'S WHO WE DIE FOR!

LOGAN!

SINCLAIR IS ORE IMPORTANT N **YOU** OR **ME.** UR LIVES ARE ORTH **NOTHING** OMPARED TO HERS!

HAVE YOU GONE **NUTS,** OLD MAN?!

RAHNE'S GOING TO BE FINE.

YOU HEAR ME, X?!

LOGAN! LET'S TAKE A WALK AND COOL OFF.

RAHNE... RAHNE...

UHN...

HI, REMEMBER ME?

HEY, RAHNE...

...HOW ARE YOU FEELING?

RRRR...

RRRRAAAA!!!...

I DO NOT UNDERSTAND.

I DO NOT UNDERSTAND.

I DO NOT UNDERSTAND.

I DO NOT UNDERSTAND.

I DO NOT HAVE CURRENT DATA ON WARPATH'S ENHANCED SENSES, AND WOLVERINE IS OUT OF HIS SENSORY RANGE.

I AM ALL THAT IS LEFT.

UNDER THE SOUNDS OF THE ATTACK, I HEAR JOSH FOLEY'S LABORED BREATHING, WHICH MEANS HE ISN'T HER TARGET...

ANGEL IS.

I HEAR THE TEARING OF MUSCLE AS IT IS SEPARATED FROM BROKEN, HOLLOW BONE AND FLESH...

HER ATTACK ON ANGEL IS NOT EMOTIONAL...IT'S STRATEGIC.

...SURGICAL.
RRRRRR...

HER SCENT, HER POSTURE, EVERYTHING ABOUT HER...SHE IS NOT GOING TO STOP.
SHE WILL HAVE TO BE--
SINCLAIR IS MORE IMPORTANT THAN YOU OR ME...
"OUR LIVES ARE WORTH NOTHING COMPARED TO HERS!"
RYAAA!!
SLIKT
SLIKT
HK!!

"SHE'S WHO WE SAVE...

SHRIPP!

"SHE'S WHY WE RISK OUR LIVES...

RRRR!

CHUK!

"SHE'S WHO WE DIE FOR."

HURR... HURR...

I HAVE THE DEMON'S WINGS.

CHICAGO.

...PROCEED AS PLANNED.

BROTHER ELI, I NEED YOU TO RENDEZVOUS WITH SINCLAIR. TAKE HER TO THE *FACILITY* BASE--A MAN NAMED *ADAM HARKIN* WILL MEET YOU THERE.

HE'S IN CHARGE OF THE *CHOIR* AND WILL BE EXPECTING YOU.

AREN'T YOU COMING?

I'LL JOIN YOU AS SOON AS I CAN. I HAVE TO GET BACK TO *THEM.*

WHAT IS IT, MATTHEW RISMAN?

THE PURIFIER ARMY. THERE IS MUCH DAY-TO-DAY BUSINESS THAT I MUST ATTEND TO.

INDEED. THE GROUNDWORK MUST BE LAID FOR WILLIAM STRYKER'S RETURN.

... THE REVEREND. YES, OF COURSE.

SOON THE REVEREND WILL TAKE CONTROL OF THE PURIFIERS AGAIN, IN PREPARATION FOR *"THE DAY."*

YOU HAVE OUR INSTRUCTIONS?

YES, *ORACLE.*

THEN YOU ARE EXCUSED.

ST. LOUIS.
A S.H.I.E.L.D. FIELD OFFICE.
WHERE HAVE I SEEN THESE WOUNDS BEFORE?
AGENT MORALES!
PURIFIER ACTIVITY. WE GOT A HIT OFF AN INTERPOL SEARCH...BUT THESE ARE SEVERAL DAYS OLD.
DAYS? HOW IS THAT POSSIBLE? WE HAVE INTERPOL DATA BEFORE THEY DO.
IT...IT LOOKS LIKE SOMEONE WIPED THE DATA FROM THE S.H.I.E.L.D. MAINFRAME. SOMEONE ON THE INSIDE.
SECURITY CAMERAS IN A GUATEMALAN JAIL CAPTURED MULTIPLE PURIFIERS BREAKING OUT THE LEPER QUEEN.
AND TRAFFIC CAMERAS CAUGHT THIS... PURIFIERS CONVERGING ON A BUILDING IN PRAGUE. THE LAST KNOWN LOCATION OF DONALD PIERCE.
BASTION'S HEAD, AN ANTI-MUTANT MILITIA LEADER, AND AN OUTLAW CYBORG...
WHATEVER THE PURIFIERS ARE UP TO, I THINK THEY'RE JUST GETTING STARTED.

FOLEY!
FOLEY!!
SMAK!
I REGAIN CONSCIOUSNESS APPROXIMATELY 7.2 MINUTES AFTER THE ASSAULT.
WOLVERINE AND WARPATH ARRIVE BEFORE MY LARYNX REFORMS.
HURKK!
YOU'VE GOT THREE SECONDS TO GET YOUR $#!^ TOGETHER, KID.
WHAT... WHAT HAP--
JOSH FOLEY, A.K.A. ELIXIR. HE WAS MY TEAMMATE AT THE XAVIER INSTITUTE, BEFORE CYCLOPS REASSIGNED ME.
TIME'S UP.
HANG ON... JUST HANG ON...
ANGEL...
I HAVE FIRSTHAND KNOWLEDGE OF HIS HEALING CAPABILITIES.
HNN...
ANGEL WILL SURVIVE.
WE SHOULD BE TRACKING WOLFSBANE RIGHT NOW.

YOU WANNA TELL US EXACTLY WHAT HAPPENED HERE?
IT WAS RAHNE...SHE WOKE UP, AND...AND EVERYTHING WAS OKAY...
...BUT THEN SHE SAW ANGEL. AND THEN...OH, GOD...THEN SHE--
I THINK WE CAN FIGURE OUT WHAT HAPPENED NEXT, FOLEY. IS WARREN GOING TO LIVE?
I'VE HEALED HIS NECK AND CHEST WOUNDS... BUT HIS WINGS...
I'LL HAVE TO RE-GROW THEM.
"WAIT... SOMETHING'S WRONG."
"WHAT IS IT, JOSH?"
"ANGEL'S WINGS..."
...THE CELLS. THEY'RE NOT HUMAN, OR MUTANT. THEY'RE NOT EVEN ORGANIC...
MY POWERS--THEY'RE NOT WORKING ON HIS WINGS. THE FOREIGN MATTER...IT'S BLOCKING ME.

HE FINALLY DID IT.
A FACILITY RED LAB. NORTH OF THE CANADA/NORTH DAKOTA BORDER. ONE AND A HALF HOURS LATER.
THE FIRST TIME STRYKER DELIVERED A PAIR OF WINGS TO THE FACILITY, I THOUGHT HE MIGHT BE INSANE. THEY WERE JUST WINGS. BIG AND RED, BUT JUST FEATHER AND BONE.
NOTHING SPECIAL.
BUT THESE... THESE ARE SPECIAL.
SO YOU FOUND THE APOCALYPSE STRAND IN THE BLOOD?
FOUND IT? EVERY CELL IN THE WINGS IS THE STRAND!
TO THE NAKED EYE, EVEN TO NORMAL MEDICAL EQUIPMENT, THESE WINGS APPEAR TO BE ORGANIC.
BUT TRUST ME...THEY ARE NOT.
YOU MAY WANT TO STEP BACK.

PLIP
LORD!
SHRACK!
WHEN THE CELLS RUN OUT OF BLOOD, THE GROWTH STOPS.
IT'S FANTASTIC.
HOW SOON CAN YOU HAVE THE TEST SUBJECT READY?
HOW SOON? I HAD HIM PREPPED BEFORE YOU LANDED. THE WAIT'S BEEN *KILLING ME.*

"YOU KNOW GABRIEL, OF COURSE. ONE OF YOUR 'SHEPHERDS.'
"HE'S VERY... COMMITTED."

I LIKE THAT ABOUT YOU PURIFIERS...THAT AND THE FACT THAT YOU'RE VERY PROMPT WITH PAYMENT.
BUT HONESTLY, TO PLAY WITH THIS KIND OF TECH? I WOULD HAVE DONE THE JOB FOR A SIGNIFICANT DISCOUNT.
PROCEED.

GABRIEL?
THIS MAY HURT A LITTLE.
PRAISE BE TO GOD.

COLORADO.
YEAARGGH!!!...
REALLY?
IT DOESN'T HURT AT ALL?
NO, SIR.
I'M ALMOST DISAPPOINTED.
YOUR DNA IS BEING REWRITTEN BY WHAT LOOKS TO BE ALIEN TECHNOLOGY, GABRIEL.
I WAS EXPECTING A LITTLE... DISCOMFORT.

AAAAAARRRGHHHH!!!...

HOLD HIM, JIMMY!!

I'M TRYING!

HE CAN'T BE THIS STRONG!!

I HAVE TO DO SOMETHING, LAURA...I HAVE TO HELP.

HE WILL NOT LET YOU. I HAVE SEEN THIS KIND O PAIN BEFORE. HE IS MORE LIKELY TO KILL YOU.

WHOA!

WARREN, STOP! WAR-- UHNN!

HURR... STOP!! MAKE IT STOP!!!

OH, CRAP.

LOOK AT HIS BACK.

I AM READY TO SERVE, FATHER.

YOU ARE THE FIRST OF OUR *CHOIR*, MY SON.
YOU WILL LEAD THE CHARGE IN STRIKING DOWN *SATAN'S SPAWN* WITH *GOD'S OWN MIGHT*.
NEED I ASK ABOUT THE REST, DOCTOR?
YOU *WOUND* ME, RISMAN.

MY GOD...
BEGIN THE INFUSIONS.
NOOOO!!

#^@%.

TALK TO ME, KID...WHAT'S HAPPENING HERE?

I...I DON'T KNOW!

"WHATEVER'S DOING THIS TO HIM...IT'S NOT STOPPING...

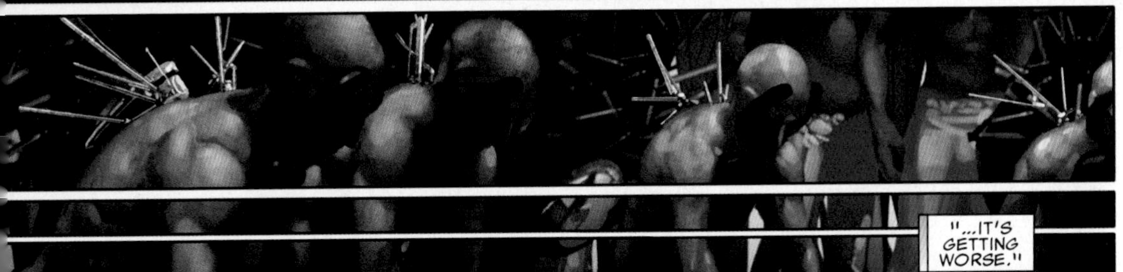

WARREN WORTHINGTON III, A.K.A. ANGEL.
A.K.A. ARCHANGEL.
WOLVERINE DID NOT INCLUDE HIM IN THE LIST OF PEOPLE WE SHOULD DIE FOR.
BUT THAT MAY NOT MATTER...

ANGEL'S AERIE. NOW.
I WAS CHOSEN BY GOD TO KILL MUTANTS.
THE LORD REACHED OUT TO ME THROUGH A MAN NAMED WILLIAM STRYKER.
NOBODY MOVE, DO YOU HEAR ME?
WARREN... WE DON'T WANT THIS, JUST RELAX AND LET THE KID HELP YOU...
HE WAS THE GREATEST MAN I HAVE EVER KNOWN.
WHAT THE $*%@ IS GOING ON HERE, LOGAN? WHAT THE HELL HAPPENED TO HIS WINGS?!

REVEREND STRYKER SAVED THE LIVES OF MY WIFE AND CHILD. HE SHOWED ME VISIONS OF THE FUTURE...
...AND SET ME ON THE PATH TO MY DESTINY.
I CAN MAKE HIM SLEEP, I JUST HAVE TO GET CLOSE--
HE CAN MAKE YOU DIE FROM FAR AWAY.
MY WINGS...I CAN FEEL THEM...

THEY TOOK MY WINGS!!!

YEARGH!!
THE REVEREND GAVE HIS LIFE TO SAVE HUMANITY FROM SATAN'S SPAWN, AND HE LEFT HIS CRUSADE IN MY HANDS.
RRRAAAA!!
FT!
FT!
I WAS GIVEN INSTRUCTIONS ON WHAT MUST BE DONE TO INSURE EDEN'S RETURN TO THE LORD, AND HOW TO KILL SATAN'S MUTANT ARMY.
GET DOWN!
AAAH!!
MY FIRST ORDER WAS TO PROTECT THE ORACLE, AS HE IS OUR ONLY CONNECTION TO THE FUTURE.
BUT LIKE OUR BELOVE REVEREND, THE ORAC WAS CUT DOWN BY THE MUTANTS.
IT HURTS... OH, GOD, IT HURTS!!
WARREN!!
GET IT TOGETHER, MAN!! DON'T MAKE ME--
SO I SOUGHT A WAY TO RESTORE HIM AND REESTABLISH HIS CONNECTION WITH THE FUTURE. AN IMPOSSIBLE TASK IF NOT FOR BROTHER ELI.
WHOAAA!
ELI FOUND ME AND LED MY PURIFIERS TO THE MEANS NECESSARY TO INFUSE THE ORACLE WITH NEW LIFE...
HUHN!
BUT NOW THAT THE ORACLE HAS BEEN REBORN IN THE FORM OF BASTION, I FEAR WE MAY HAVE HANDED HUMANITY OVER TO A NEW EVIL.

MAKE IT STOP!!
ARRGH!!..
JIMMY!!
SAFEGUARDING THE ORACLE WAS ONLY ONE OF THE TWO MISSIONS GIVEN TO ME BY REVEREND STRYKER...
MAKE IT STOP!!
THE OTHER WAS TO BUILD A CHOIR OF HUMAN ANGELS USING ALIEN TECHNOLOGY HIDDEN WITHIN THE ANGELIC WINGS OF AN UNKNOWN MUTANT.
OKAY, BUB. WHATEVER YOU WANT--
WARREN!!...
CRASH!!
WE DISCOVERED TWO MUTANTS WITH FEATHERED WINGS, BUT IT WAS THE ONE CALLED "ANGEL" THAT HELD THE TECHNOLOGY WE NEEDED.

THE FACILITY.
NOW REVEREND STRYKER'S CHOIR AWAITS MY ORDERS AND READIES FOR THE COMING WAR.
MY NAME IS MATTHEW RISMAN AND TODAY I FIGHT FOR THE LORD...
AND FOR MY FRIEND, WILLIAM STRYKER.
BASTION HAS DEFILED THE REVEREND'S BODY WITH HIS TECHNO-ORGANIC PLAGUE AND HIS EVERY ACTION IS AN ASSAULT AGAINST OUR HOLY CRUSADE.
ORACLE OR NOT, HE MUST BE STOPPED. NOW.
MATTHEW, WHAT DO YOU PLAN TO DO?
FIRST, I WILL PUT WILLIAM'S SOUL TO REST.
THEN, I WILL DESTROY THE TECHNO-ORGANIC MONSTER BASTION CALLS "MAGUS."
AND THEN I WILL KILL THE ORACLE.
BROTHER ELI, I THANK YOU FOR YOUR LOYALTY, AND YOUR FAITH.
REVEREND CRAIG, YOU'VE SERVED THE LORD WELL. NOW I NEED YOU TO FINISH YOUR WORK AND RETURN WOLFSBANE TO SATAN.
I LOOK FORWARD TO OUR NEXT MEETING...HERE, OR IN THE PRESENCE OF THE LORD.
MATTHEW...

MATTHEW, *WAIT!!*
I WANT TO COME WITH YOU.
ELI...BASTION HAS STRYKER, AND STRYKER COMMANDS THE PURIFIERS.
THE ONLY REASON THE CHOIR IS STILL FOLLOWING MY ORDERS IS BECAUSE THEY DON'T KNOW OF STRYKER'S "*RESURRECTION.*"
I HAVE FAITH, BUT I AM ALSO A PRACTICAL MAN. WE MAY NOT BE COMING BACK.
I BROUGHT THIS EVIL ON YOU. I GAVE YOU BASTION'S LOCATION.
THIS IS MY RESPONSIBILITY.
ELI...
WE ARE BROTHERS, YOU SAID SO YOURSELF. WE SHOULD FINISH THIS FIGHT TOGETHER.
...
THANK YOU, ELI.
NOW COME...

"...OUR DESTINY AWAITS."

CHICAGO.
"WE CALLED HIM 'SON,' 'BROTHER.' 'FATHER.'
"BUT NOW HE IS LOST."
SEDUCED BY THE DEVIL.
HE HAS BETRAYED EVERYTHING WE HOLD SACRED.
EVER SINCE MY RESURRECTION, I'VE KNOWN OF THE JUDAS IN OUR MIDST.
THAT JUDAS IS MATTHEW RISMAN.
THAT JUDAS IS MATTHEW RISMAN.
NOW HE IS COMING TO KILL US ALL. TO DELIVER US UNTO SATAN.
NOW HE IS COMING TO KILL US ALL. TO DELIVER US UNTO SATAN!
MATTHEW RISMAN MUST BE STRUCK DOWN.
MATTHEW RISMAN MUST BE STRUCK DOWN.

THE FACILITY.

NO!

YE ARE SATAN'S SPAWN.
GIVE IN TO YUIR TRUE NATURE.
INSIDE YE IS THE BEAST.
LET IT OUT.
LET IT FEAST.
YE ARE EVIL THROUGH AND THROUGH, RAHNE SINCLAIR. YE KNOW THIS. YE HAVE ALWAYS KNOWN. NOW YE CAN LET IT OUT.
GIVE IN TO THE BEAST INSIDE YE.

PLEASE, LORD...PLEASE LET ME WAKE UP...
NONO NONONONO... PLEASE...I DIDN'T MEAN TO...
PLEASE PLEASE PLEASE...
HEAVENLY FATHER, PLEASE FORGIVE ME...
NAE. THERE IS NO FORGIVENESS FOR DEMONS.
THERE IS ONLY WRATH.

OVER MID-AMERICA.
I KNOW WE'RE IN A @#$% ING JET, BUT IF HE GOES ANY FASTER, WE'RE GONNA LOSE HIM.
HE'S TURNING.
STAY ON HIM, JIMMY...
I GOT IT.
HE WAS PREVIOUSLY HEADING NORTH-NORTHEAST, NOW HE IS HEADING DUE EAST.
HIS TARGET IS MOVING.
THE PURIFIERS MADE RAHNE TAKE HIS WINGS.
EVEN MONEY SAYS WARREN'S GOING AFTER THEM.

THE REVEREND WILLIAM STRYKER LEFT US TO FINISH HIS CRUSADE...
BUT TO THIS, WE MUST FIGHT EVERY BATTLE THE LORD SETS BEFORE US.
TODAY, WE FACE A BETRAYER WITHIN OUR OWN RANKS AND ONCE HE IS DEAD, NOTHING WILL PROTECT THE MUTANTS FROM GOD'S WRATH.
GABRIEL, DO YOU COPY?
YES, FATHER?
WE'RE APPROACHING THE SITE NOW. THEY'LL HAVE EYES IN PLACE ON THE ROOF.
BLIND THEM.
UNDERSTOOD.
MICHAEL, DANIEL...CLEAR A PATH.

UT!
HR!

WH-WHY DID YOU MAKE ME HURT MY FRIENDS?
WHY HAVE YOU DONE THIS TO ME?
BECAUSE YE TWISTED MY THOUGHTS...YE MADE ME BELIEVE THAT YUIR EVIL WAS IN ME.
BUT THE TRUTH IS YE ARE THE DEVIL'S DAUGHTER...
SATAN IS YUIR FATHER, AND I AM YUIR EXECUTIONER.
BLAM
AAAAHHH!

THUD!
HNN!!
HNN...I'M... SORRY...ALL I...NN!!
...ALL I EVER WANTED... WAS YOUR... LOVE...
...NOT THIS...
RRRRRRR
AAAHHH!
RAAA!!
NO!! YE WON'T FIND SALVATION THAT WAY!
THERE IS NOTHING LEFT FOR YE BUT ETERNAL DAMNATION!

I WALK AMONG MY FALLEN BROTHERS, LED TO THEIR GRAVES BY THE LIES OF THE ORACLE.

HIS UNHOLY ATROCITIES NOT ONLY ENDANGER THE LIVES OF EVERY GOD-FEARING MAN, WOMAN AND CHILD ON THE PLANET...

...BUT OUR VERY SOULS.

A PRICE TOO HIGH TO PAY FOR THE DESTRUCTION OF *SATAN'S ARMY*...

BUT AN EASY SACRIFICE FOR ONE *WITHOUT* A SOUL.

BASTION.

A WORD, IF YOU WILL.

6

CHICAGO,
14 HOURS AGO.
"OKAY, LOGAN TAKE ME THROUGH IT AGAIN."
"LIKE I SAID, SUMMERS... I DON'T KNOW EXACTLY WHAT HAPPENED BEFORE WE GOT THERE, BUT WHATEVER WENT DOWN...
"...IT WAS REAL @#$% ING BAD."
STAND DOWN, MATTHEW RISMAN. THIS WILL ACCOMPLISH NOTHING. OUR END GOAL IS THE SAME...PRESERVATION OF HUMANITY AGAINST THE MUTANT THREAT.
YOU'RE WRONG, BASTION. WE'RE NOTHING ALIKE. BECAUSE YOU'RE NOT HUMAN.
"MY GUESS IS THAT RISMAN WAS IN SOME KIND OF FIGHT TO MAINTAIN CONTROL OF THE PURIFIERS..."
THEY'RE NOT HUMAN.
"AND HE WAS LOSING THAT FIGHT... BADLY."
THOSE UNHOLY ABOMINATIONS YOU'VE CREATED WILL BE DESTROYED.
BUT NOT BEFORE YOU FACE THE WRATH OF GOD'S CHOIR.
"AND THINGS WERE ABOUT TO GET A LOT WORSE FOR HIM."
CRASH!!!
WHAT IN--?

"NOW, I DIDN'T GET MUCH INFO FROM ANGEL WHEN HE WAS TRYING TO KILL US, BUT I DID KNOW WHAT HE WAS AFTER..."
RRYYAAA!!
"...HIS WINGS."
ELI, MOVE!!
GIVE THEM BACK!!
"AND SOMEHOW HE KNEW THE PURIFIERS HAD 'EM."
AAARRGHH!!
AAIIIEEEE!!
GIVE THEM BACK!!

"WHEN HE FINALLY CAUGHT UP TO THEM, HE HAD ABOUT FIFTY SETS TO CHOSE FROM."
FATHER... IS THAT...IS THAT ONE OF US?
NO...SATAN IS PLAYING HIS TRICKS. IT'S WORTHINGTON. HE'S A MUTANT, GABRIEL...
KILL HIM.
"AND BY THE LOOKS OF THINGS...
"...HE WANTED THEM ALL."
AAAAAHH!
NYEARGHH!!
THE X-MEN ARE COMING FOR YOU, MATTHEW RISMAN. WE TOLD YOU ALREADY HOW THIS WOULD END.
I'VE MADE MY PEACE WITH GOD. I'M READY TO DIE.
BUT YOU GO FIRST!

"LUCKY FOR US, THESE GUYS WERE SO FOCUSED ON KILLING EACH OTHER, THEY DIDN'T SEE US COMING."
SHRACK!!
RRRRRRAAAA!!
<<<SQUARRRRKK>>>
"BUT THAT DIDN'T CHANGE THE FACT WE WERE IN OVER OUR HEADS."
WHAT THE HELL IS GOING ON HERE? WHO ARE THESE GUYS? IS THAT...IS THAT BASTION?!
FORTY-EIGHT TARGETS, INCLUDING AIRBORNE.
GREAT, SO WHAT'S THE PLAN?
SIXTEEN APIECE.
KILL 'EM ALL.

THE FACILITY.
"SO, WHILE WE WERE FIGHTING BASTION AND A $#!% LOAD OF FLYING PURIFIERS..."
SATAN'S SPAWN CAN NEVER HIDE FROM THE RIGHTEOUS!
"...RAHNE WAS BATTLING HER OWN DEMONS."
YUIR TAINTED BLOOD BETRAYS YE.
"WE KNOW REVEREND CRAIG JOINED THE PURIFIERS IN ORDER TO LURE RAHNE INTO A TRAP."
NOW I CAN FINALLY FINISH WHAT MOIRA MACTAGGERT STOPPED ME FROM DOING SO LONG AGO!
"AND ONCE HE CAPTURED HER, THE PURIFIERS PROGRAMMED RAHNE TO CHEW OFF WARREN'S WINGS."
COME OUT, DEMON!
"BUT THAT WASN'T THE SICKEST PART OF THIS WHOLE DEAL...
COME OUT SO I CAN--
EH?

"THE SICKEST PART IS THAT CRAIG ONLY AGREED TO DO WHAT THE PURIFIERS WANTED IF HE WAS ALLOWED TO KILL RAHNE WHEN IT WAS OVER."

GRRRRAAA!

AAAH!!

WHAM!

YOU *DARE* CALL ME A DEMON AFTER WHAT YOU'VE DONE?!

UHN!!

YOU TOOK GOD'S WORD AND TWISTED IT, YOU TOOK SOMETHING PURE AND HOLY AND USED IT TO JUSTIFY TORTURE AND MURDER.

YOU ARE THE DEMON, NOT ME.

I NEVER WANTED ANY OF THIS. I NEVER WANTED TO HURT YOU.

I ONLY CAME AFTER YOU TO SAVE YOU FROM THE PURIFIERS.

I CAME BECAUSE YOU ARE MY FATHER...AND BECAUSE PART OF ME STILL LOVED YOU.

BUT NOW, AFTER WHAT YOU'VE DONE... AFTER WHAT YOU MADE ME DO...

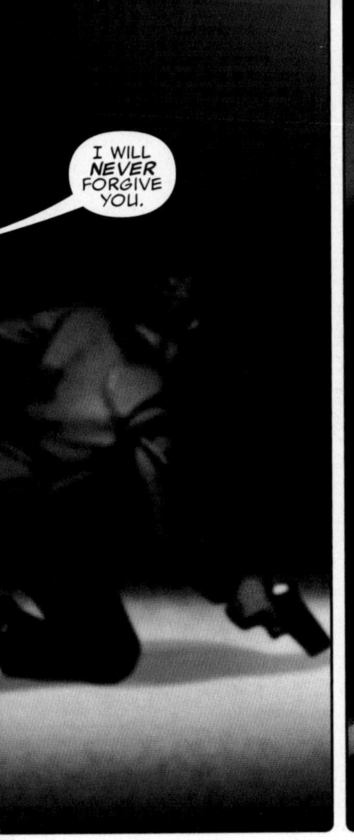

AND IT IS TIME YE RETURN TO HIM!

GASP
KILL THE ANGEL.
RRRAAAAA!!
AAAAHH!!

ACK AT THE HANGAR, ANGEL WAS
CING UP THOSE FLYING PURIFIERS
A PRETTY GOOD CLIP AND FOR
MOMENT, IT FELT LIKE WARREN
WAS ON OUR SIDE."
AACK!!
GOOD THING, TOO, BECAUSE X-23 AND WARPATH WERE HAVING A HELL OF A TIME MAKING A DENT IN THEIR NUMBERS FROM THE GROUND."
GUH!!
CHUK!
AAAIIEEE!!
"BUT IT WASN'T FOR LACK OF TRYING."
THUD!
THUD!
SNFF
RISMAN.
X!? X, WAIT! WHERE ARE YOU GOING?!
AAARGHH!
CHUK!!
"NOW THIS IS WHERE THINGS GET WEIRD.

"REMEMBER HOW I SAID I THOUGHT RISMAN WAS IN SOME KIND OF POWER STRUGGLE?"

MAGUS!!! TIME TO FACE THE WRATH OF--

"TURNS OUT IT MAY NOT HAVE BEEN JUST WITH BASTION."

...ELI?

MATTHEW. I HOPED YOU MIGHT FIND ME.

DEAR GOD... ELI, GET AWAY FROM THAT CREATURE!

THERE IS NO GOD, YOU FOOL...THERE'S ONLY ***DEATH.***
AND SHE IS MY QUEEN.

NO... NO!!
THAT WASN'T VERY NICE.
I TRUSTED YOU! I BELIEVED IN YOU!!
THAT WAS A MISTAKE...ONE OF MANY YOU'VE MADE.
I WAS GOING TO MAKE AN OFFERING OF YOU AND YOUR ENTIRE PURIFIER ARMY. YOUR SOULS WERE TO BE REAPED AS SUSTENANCE FOR MY BELOVED...
BUT ONCE I SAW WHAT THIS CREATURE WAS CAPABLE OF, I CHANGED MY PLANS.
NOW YOU'RE JUST GOING TO DIE.
GOD... FORGIVE ME...

"WE DIDN'T FIND OUT MUCH ABOUT THE MYSTERY MAN THAT WAS TRYING TO KILL RISMAN...
"...BECAUSE LAURA GOT TO THE SCENE FIRST.
MATTHEW?
"SHE PUT ONE ROUND IN RISMAN'S HEAD AND THREE ROUNDS IN THIS OTHER GUY...
"...BUT THE BULLETS WENT RIGHT THROUGH HIM.
"OR HE WENT RIGHT THROUGH THEM... EITHER WAY, THIS GUY SURE AS HELL WASN'T A PURIFIER."
SSSS...

I SHOULD JUST KILL YOU NOW FOR DENYING ME MATTHEW'S SOUL...
...BUT I CAN'T RESIST THE MEAL YOUR HEALING FACTOR OFFERS.
SO MUCH LIFE TO OFFER... AND NOW WITH MAGUS BONDED TO ME, I HAVE TWO MOUTHS TO FEED.
NNYEAARGHH!
HK!!
I'LL BRING YOU TO THE BRINK OF DEATH AND THEN YOU'LL COME BACK TO ME.
HNNNNN...
AGAIN. AND AGAIN. AND AGAIN...
THOK!
AAAHHH!

"FORTUNATELY, THAT'S ABOUT THE TIME JIMMY SHOWED UP."
DROP HER, OR YOU'RE DEAD.
TOO LATE. I'M ALREADY DEAD, APACHE.
KILL... HIM...
I'VE KILLED MORE OF YOUR KIND THAN SMALLPOX, JAMES PROUDSTAR...
...AND YOU'VE JUST MADE THIS **PERSONAL.**
YOU OKAY?
YEAH...
DID...DID I COMPLETE MY MISSION?
...YOU DID GOOD, LAURA.
NOW LET'S GET YOU OUT OF HERE.

"I DIDN'T GET AN EXACT
OUNT OF HOW MANY PURIFIERS
WARREN TOOK OUT..."
"FROM THE SNARES OF THE DEVIL, DELIVER US, OH LORD."
"BUT WE DIDN'T FIND ANY LEFT ALIVE."
DO NOT FALTER.
DO NOT FEAR.
GABRIEL... WE MUST GO...
GABRIEL... HE IS COMING.
"OR IN ONE PIECE, FOR THAT MATTER."
THE ANGEL OF DEATH IS COMING FOR US.
GOD SAVE OUR SOULS.
"SO, IF ANY OF THEM GOT OUT, I DIDN'T KNOW ABOUT IT...

"...I HAD MY HANDS FULL."
SHRACK!
STAY! DOWN!
"THE WHOLE TIME, THE ONLY QUESTION THAT RAN THROUGH MY HEAD WAS HOW MANY TIMES DO WE HAVE TO KILL THESE BASTARDS BEFORE THEY STAY DEAD?"
YOUR SPECIES HAS BROUGHT THIS ON ITSELF, WOLVERINE. EVERY ONE OF YOU HAS THE POTENTIAL TO DESTROY HUMANITY...
...AND THAT WE CANNOT ALLOW.
ARRGH!
WE PLANNED ON YOUR TEAM KILLING MATTHEW RISMAN, BUT THIS CONFRONTATION IS PREMATURE.
I DON'T KNOW HOW YOU CAME BACK, BUB, AND I DON'T CARE. CUZ I'M GONNA SEND YOU BACK TO WHATEVER ROBOT HELL YOU CAME FROM.

"NOW I'VE SEEN A LOT OF @#$%ED UP STUFF IN MY DAY, BUT THIS...
"THIS I COULDN'T BELIEVE."
NO...
"IT WAS LIKE SEEING EVERY SKELETON IN THE X-MEN CLOSET BACK FROM THE DEAD."
NO @#$% ING WAY.
"THAT SAID, I REALLY SHOULD HAVE KEPT MY FOCUS ON BASTION."
KRA-KOOM!

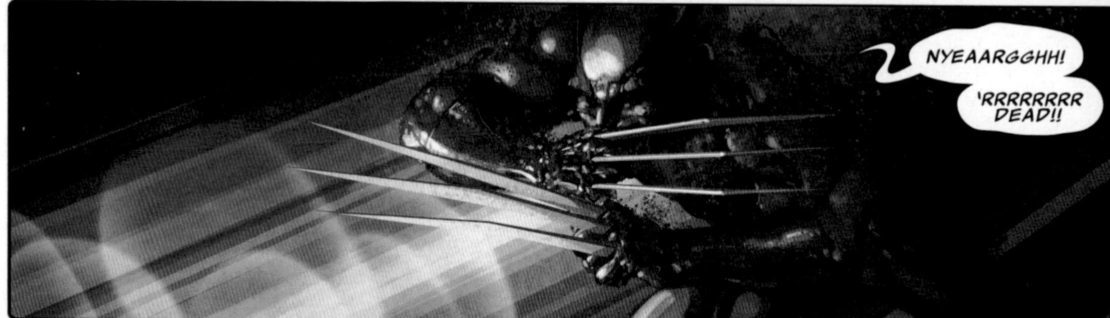

DO YOU HEAR ME?!

DO YOU HEAR ME?!!

RISK ANALYSIS...

...UNACCEPTABLE.
DAMMIT!
PROBLEM, BASTION?
YES. WE ARE ABANDONING THIS BASE, CAMERON HODGE.
WILLIAM STRYKER, PREPARE FOR TAKEOFF.
OF COURSE, BASTION.
COME ON, COME ON, MOVE DAMMIT!
MOVE!! MO--
"IN THE END WE TOOK OUT RISMAN...

"...BUT THERE'S A CRAP LOAD OF TROUBLE THAT GOT AWAY."
DAMN BUT YOU SMELL, OLD MAN.
YES. VERY BAD.
SHUT UP, BOTH OF YOU, AND TAKE A GOOD LOOK.
THIS IS WHAT YOU SIGNED UP FOR.
THIS IS YOUR LIFE NOW, AND THE BLOOD NEVER COMES OFF.
NOW WHERE IS HE?
OVER THERE...BUT YOU'RE NOT GONNA BELIEVE IT.
AFTER WHAT I'VE SEEN TODAY, DON'T BE SO SURE.
OKAY, I TAKE IT BACK.
"SEEING ALL THE ENEMIES I THOUGHT WE'D BEATEN AND BURIED BACK IN THE FLESH IS SOMETHING I WON'T FORGET ANYTIME SOON.

"JUST LIKE SEEING WARREN LYING ON TOP OF A BLOODY PILE OF MURDER HE COMMITTED.
"THESE ARE THINGS I JUST NEVER CONTEMPLATED.

"BUT IT'S THE IMAGE OF RAHNE, SOAKED IN THE BLOOD OF HER FATHER, PRAYING FOR FORGIVENESS, THAT I CAN'T SHAKE."
THERE IS NO SIN SO TERRIBLE THAT GOD'S LOVE CANNOT FORGIVE...
"SHE WON'T TALK ABOUT WHAT HAPPENED...HELL, SHE WON'T TALK AT ALL."
THERE IS NO SIN SO TERRIBLE THAT GOD'S LOVE CANNOT FORGIVE...
"BUT WE DIDN'T FIND A BODY...JUST A LOT OF BLOOD AND THE OLD BASTARD'S CLOTHES."
THERE IS NO SIN SO TERRIBLE THAT GOD'S LOVE CANNOT FORGIVE...
"GOD HELP HER ONCE THE SHOCK WEARS OFF..."
THERE IS NO SIN...
"...AND SHE REMEMBERS WHAT SHE DID."
THERE IS NO...

AS FOR WORTHINGTON, HE DIDN'T HAVE A SCRATCH ON HIM, LIKE IT NEVER HAPPENED.
"BUT HE SAID THAT THOSE WINGS ARE STILL INSIDE HIM...AND THAT THEY WANT TO COME OUT AGAIN.
"ELIXIR CONFIRMED. HE'S CHANGED, FOR GOOD.
"SINCLAIR'S HEALED UP NOW. PHYSICALLY, SHE'S FINE.
HER HURT IS DEEPER THAN THAT.
WE'LL DO EVERYTHING WE CAN FOR RAHNE AND WARREN.
BUT WE CAN'T STOP WHAT WE'VE STARTED. NOT AFTER WHAT YOU'VE JUST TOLD ME.
AND YOU HAVE NO IDEA WHO KILLED THE TECHNARCH? THE MAN WARPATH AND X-23 SAW?
X-23 HEARD THE NAME "ELI" BEFORE EVERYTHING WENT SIDEWAYS. THAT'S ALL WE'VE GOT.
THEN I'VE ONLY GOT ONE MORE QUESTION TO ASK.

WHO'S NEXT?

HATE THAT_

'NUFF TO DRIVE A MAN CRAZY, HUH?
SEEIN' YOUR HANDS ARE OCCUPIED, HOW 'BOUT I TAKE CARE OF THAT FOR YOU?

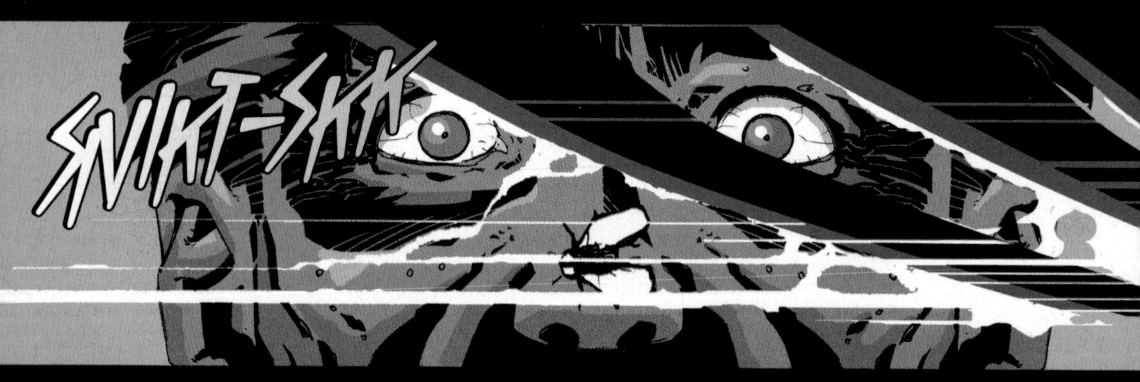
SNIKT-SKK

THERE, THAT'S BETTER_

AIN'T IT, BUB?

IN'T NO DOG
NOTHIN' WORSE THAN HAVIN' A ITCH YA JUST CAN'T SCRATCH.
MURFLM-MMUMH.
MAN, THESE THINGS ARE SLIPPERY. TELL YA, EASY ENOUGH TO TALK ABOUT HEALIN' FACTORS AN' ALL, BUT THESE BUGGERS DON'T PUT THEMSELVES BACK INSIDE.
EVER SEEN SKIN HEAL AROUND A YARD OR TWO OF INTESTINE STICKIN' OUT YER BELLY?

FRSLLLTCH
TRUST ME, IT'S NASTY.
DON'T 'SPOSE YOU GOT A BABY WIPE?
SORRY 'BOUT THIS. NOT THAT I'M PRISSY 'BOUT THE STUFF. JUST IT DRIES AND CLOGS THE CLAW SOCKETS IN MY GLOVES.
Hmmm, WHAT HAVE WE HERE?

TELL YA, THERE WAS A TIME, SITUATION LIKE WE GOT HERE, I WOULDA JUST 'BOUT KILLED FOR ONE 'A THESE COFFIN NAILS.
AH, WHO'M I KIDDIN'.
BEEN TIMES I HAVE KILLED FOR ONE.
BUT NOT NO MORE. GOT RIDDA THAT MONKEY.
'SIDES.
GOT PLENTY BETTER THINGS TO KILL FOR THESE DAYS.
SNIKT
"CUTE."

NOT HOW I'D DESCRIBE IT.

YEAH, WELL, YOU'RE A HUMORLESS ####, AIN'T YA?

AND YA AIN'T THE ONE GOIN' OUT ON THIS, ARE YA?

YEAH, I KNOW, WHY THE #### SHOULD I CARE?
NOT LIKE I HAVEN'T DONE IT BEFORE.
YOU WANT THE TEAM FOR THIS?
I TAKE IT BACK.
YOU'RE NOT HUMORLESS.
BUT YOU'RE STILL A ####.

WELL, LOGAN--
I WOULDN'T WANT YOU TO BE THE ONLY #### IN THE ROOM.
SSST
AFTER YOU.
NOW WHO'S THE ONLY #### IN THE ROOM, BUB?

I'M SERIOUS ABOUT THE BACKUP. I COULD SEND PIXIE WITH YOU.
Oh, HAR-HAR-HAR-DEE HAR-HAR.
LOOKING FOR SOMETHING IN YOUR JACKET?
Huh?
Oh. NAW.
JUST I'VE HAD SO MANY BAD HABITS OVER THE YEARS. A MISSION LIKE THIS COMES AROUND--
--AND I FORGET WHICH ONES I QUIT.
"Oh NO, NOT AGAIN."

KRASH
SNIKT
LOOKS LIKE YOUR FRIENDS ARE BACK.

KILL
KILL
KILL
Ah, HELL.

KILL KILL KILL
KILL KILL
KILL KILL
KILL
KILL
KILL
KILL
klik
GRNNK
KILL
KILL
KILL
KILL
KILL
KILL
KILL
KILL
KILL KILL KILL
KILL
KILL
KILL KILL
KILL

KILL
KILL
KILL
BUB, YOU GOTTA TELL ME SOMETIME--
FZZZZT
KILL KILL
KILL
KRNCHH
KILL
KILL
KILL
KILL
KILL KILL
KILL KILL
KILL
KILL
KILL
HOW'S IT FEEL BEIN' SO WANTED?
MUPHINGUH!

Ah, CRAP.
KILL
KILL
KILL
KILL
KILL
KILL
Ahhh, CRAAAP.
KILL
KILL
KILL
KILL
LOOK, I'M GONNA HAVE TO DO SOMETHING 'BOUT THIS.
KILL
KILL
I'D SAY IT'S BEEN GOOD TA KNOW YA--
KILL
KILL
KILL
BUT I'D BE LYIN' LIKE A DOG.

KILL
KILL
KILL
KILL
KILL
KILL
AN' I AIN'T NO DOG-
JEEZUS-
KILL
KILL
KILL
JEE-ZUS!
KILL
KILL
SWEET JEEZUS-
KILL
KILL

JEEZUS, I LOVE THIS.
KILL
KILL
KILL
KILL
KILL
KILL
KILL
KILL
KILL

THEY AIN'T INNOCENT...

MEAN TA SAY, NONE OF US IS INNOCENT.
NOT THESE PATHETIC PSYCHOS.
AND LEASTWAYS, NOT ME.
ME, I CAN'T SPELL INNOCENT WITHOUT I GOT A DICTIONARY TO LOOK IT UP.

BUT YA
ASK ME--
SOME ARE
A LITTLE
LIGHTER ON
THE WHOLE
INNOCENCE
THING THAN
OTHERS.
SOME SLOBS,
THEY GOT MAYBE
A LITTLE LESS IN
THE TANK THAN
MOST.

NOT THAT I'M ONE TA JUDGE WHOSE HANDS ARE CLEAN.

KILL
KILL

KILL
KILL
KILL

KILL KILL

KILL
KILL
KI--

NAK-AKAKAKAKKKT

TELL YA, BUB, THIS WAS SOME KINDA SHOW YA PUT ON HERE.

MEAN TA SAY--

I'VE HAD SOME TRAPS SPRUNG ON ME, BUT THIS WAS A DOOZY.
MUNH? MO! MO!
NAW, DON'T GO RUININ' A PERFECT RELATIONSHIP WITH LIES, BUB.
SEE, SUMMERS, HE MAY BE A ####, BUT HE'S GOT WAYS 'A KNOWIN' THINGS.
LIKE 'BOUT THAT CHIP IN YOUR HEAD. LIKE HOW IT BROADCASTS A SIGNATURE TO CEREBRO THAT LOOKS JUST LIKE A MUTANT.
A NEW MUTANT.
TREASURE.
AN' 'BOUT HOW THESE SLOBS VOLUNTEERED. GET INJECTED WITH A NANOCHIP THAT LODGES IN THEIR BRAINS. LETS 'EM BE CONTROLLED BY THE MASTER CHIP IN YOUR NOGGIN.

HOW THEY VOLUNTEERED TO LET YOU TURN 'EM INTO BERSERKERS.
HOW YOUR BOSS PROMISED 'EM A SPECIAL PARADISE FOR THEIR SACRIFICE.
ELL, YA PLAYED IT GOOD, BUB. ADE IT LOOK LIKE THEY HAD . MADE IT LOOK LIKE THEY AS COMIN' FOR YA. BUT EN IF THE #### HADN'T T ME IN ON THE DEAL, D 'A KNOWN WHAT AS UP.
SEE, YA NEVER SMELLED AFRAID, BUB.
NOT LIKE YA DO NOW, ANYWAY.

WELL, GOOD NEWS IS--
SUMMERS SAYS HE NEEDS THAT CHIP INTACT.
BAD NEWS IS--
HE LEFT IT TO **ME** HOW TA GET MY HANDS ON IT.
SNKTT-KT

YA MIND, BUB?
'COURSE YA DON'T.
AH, CRAP.
BETTER NOT.
THE KITTEN, SHE'D COME BACK AN' KILL ME IF SHE KNEW I DID SOMETHIN' THAT BAD.
The End

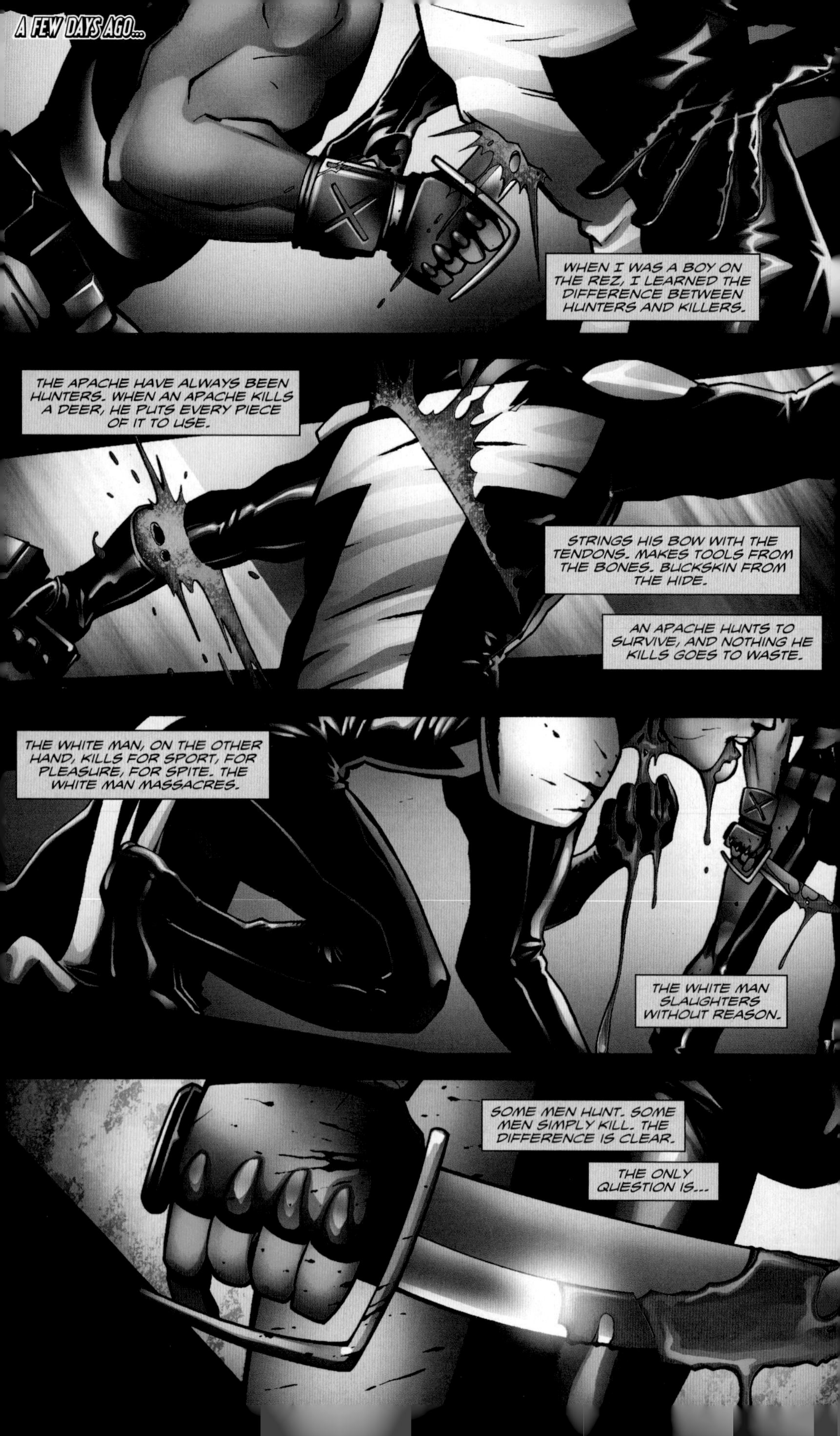
A FEW DAYS AGO...
WHEN I WAS A BOY ON THE REZ, I LEARNED THE DIFFERENCE BETWEEN HUNTERS AND KILLERS.
THE APACHE HAVE ALWAYS BEEN HUNTERS. WHEN AN APACHE KILLS A DEER, HE PUTS EVERY PIECE OF IT TO USE.
STRINGS HIS BOW WITH THE TENDONS. MAKES TOOLS FROM THE BONES. BUCKSKIN FROM THE HIDE.
AN APACHE HUNTS TO SURVIVE, AND NOTHING HE KILLS GOES TO WASTE.
THE WHITE MAN, ON THE OTHER HAND, KILLS FOR SPORT, FOR PLEASURE, FOR SPITE. THE WHITE MAN MASSACRES.
THE WHITE MAN SLAUGHTERS WITHOUT REASON.
SOME MEN HUNT. SOME MEN SIMPLY KILL. THE DIFFERENCE IS CLEAR.
THE ONLY QUESTION IS...

WHICH ONE
HAVE I BECOME?
HUNTERS
& KILLERS

ANGEL'S AERIE, COLORADO.
NOW.

GRIZZLY BEAR. 12,000 POUNDS OF HIM. ONLY A COUPLE MINUTES AHEAD OF ME.
LAST NIGHT IT KILLED A STRAY DOG I'D TAKEN IN. GUTTED IT. RIPPED IT TO SHREDS.
PART OF ME WANTS TO BE THE HUNTER. TO BE TRUE TO THE OLD WAYS.
BUT BEAR MEAT IS LOADED WITH PARASITES. IT'S A PAIN IN THE ASS TO PREPARE.
AND I GOT NO USE FOR TRINKETS MADE OF BONE OR CLAW.
PART OF ME JUST WANTS TO SEE IT DIE.
AS IF I DON'T HAVE ENOUGH DEATHS ON MY CONSCIENCE ALREADY.

I KNOW HOW TO KILL. WITH A KNIFE. WITH MY HANDS. LOGAN AND CABLE BOTH SAW TO THAT OVER THE YEARS.
BUT WHAT THEY NEVER TAUGHT ME WAS HOW TO LIVE WITH MYSELF AFTERWARDS.
WHENEVER I CLOSE MY EYES, I SEE THEM.
THERE WAS THE GUY IN WICHITA WHOSE EYES STRETCHED WIDE WITH TERROR AS HE MUMBLED A FINAL, FUTILE PRAYER.
THERE WAS THE BOY IN TULSA WHO WAS BARELY OLD ENOUGH TO SHAVE. HE COUGHED UP BLOOD AS HE HISSED A CURSE.
I REMEMBER THEM GOING SLACK BENEATH MY KNIFE. REMEMBER THE DEATH RATTLES. THE NAMES THEY CRIED. THE HELLS THEY DAMNED ME TO.
I REMEMBER EACH ONE IN VIVID DETAIL.
I TELL MYSELF, I DID THE RIGHT THING. THEY'RE PURIFIERS. THEY'RE IN THE BUSINESS OF KILLING MUTANTS. IT WAS THEM OR ME.
BUT THAT DOESN'T MAKE THE BURDEN ANY EASIER TO BEAR.

MAYBE SOME DAY I'LL BE ABLE TO LAY THAT BURDEN DOWN. MAYBE SOME DAY I CAN--
SNAP
RRAAR
UUHH!
STUPID, JAMES. REALLY STUPID.
RRAAARGGG

GRAAAA
RRAAAAAAAR
SHUNK

THERE ARE HUNTERS AND THERE ARE KILLERS. THE DIFFERENCE IS CLEAR.
BUT SOMETIMES A HUNTER CAN LOSE HIS WAY.
ALL RIGHT THEN, YOU BASTARD. PICK ON SOMEONE YOUR OWN SIZE FOR A CHANGE.
SOMETIMES WHEN HE'S HURT, HE'LL LASH OUT.
WHEN HE'S THREATENED, HE'LL KILL ANYTHING THAT STANDS IN HIS WAY.
AND IF NO ONE'S EVER THERE TO HELP HIM, HE MAY LOSE HIS WAY FOREVER...
AND FORGET THE MAN HE WAS.

MY NAME IS JAMES PROUDSTAR, AND I KILL BECAUSE I'M FIGHTING FOR SELF-PRESERVATION. FIGHTING FOR A BETTER WORLD.
EASY THERE, BIG FELLA. I'M NOT GONNA HURT YOU.
ONCE THAT FIGHT IS WON, I PRAY I'LL BE ABLE TO HANG UP THESE KNIVES FOREVER.
ONCE THE WORLD IS AT PEACE, MAYBE I CAN FINALLY TAKE THE TIME TO FIGURE OUT EXACTLY WHAT IT IS I'M SUPPOSED TO BE.
THUNDERBIRD. HELLION. WARPATH. X-MAN. APACHE. MUTANT. SOLDIER.
HUNTER OR KILLER OR NONE OF THE ABOVE.
BUT BEFORE I EVER GET TO THAT POINT, BEFORE I'LL EVER HAVE THE LUXURY OF PEACE, I KNOW ONE THING FOR SURE...

THERE'S STILL A LOT MORE KILLING TO BE DONE.
JAMES. TIME TO SUIT UP, BOY.
ASSUMING YOU STILL GOT THE HEART FOR THIS.
IF NOT, TELL ME NOW.
JUST HOLD YOUR DAMN HORSES, LOGAN.
WHAT'S ALL THAT FOR?
THERE'S ONE NOTCH FOR EACH OF THEM.
ONE FOR EVERY MAN I'VE KILLED.

YOU WON'T.

END.

WE'RE DOING THIS QUICK AND CLEAN.
I'LL CALL YOU IN IF I NEED YOU.

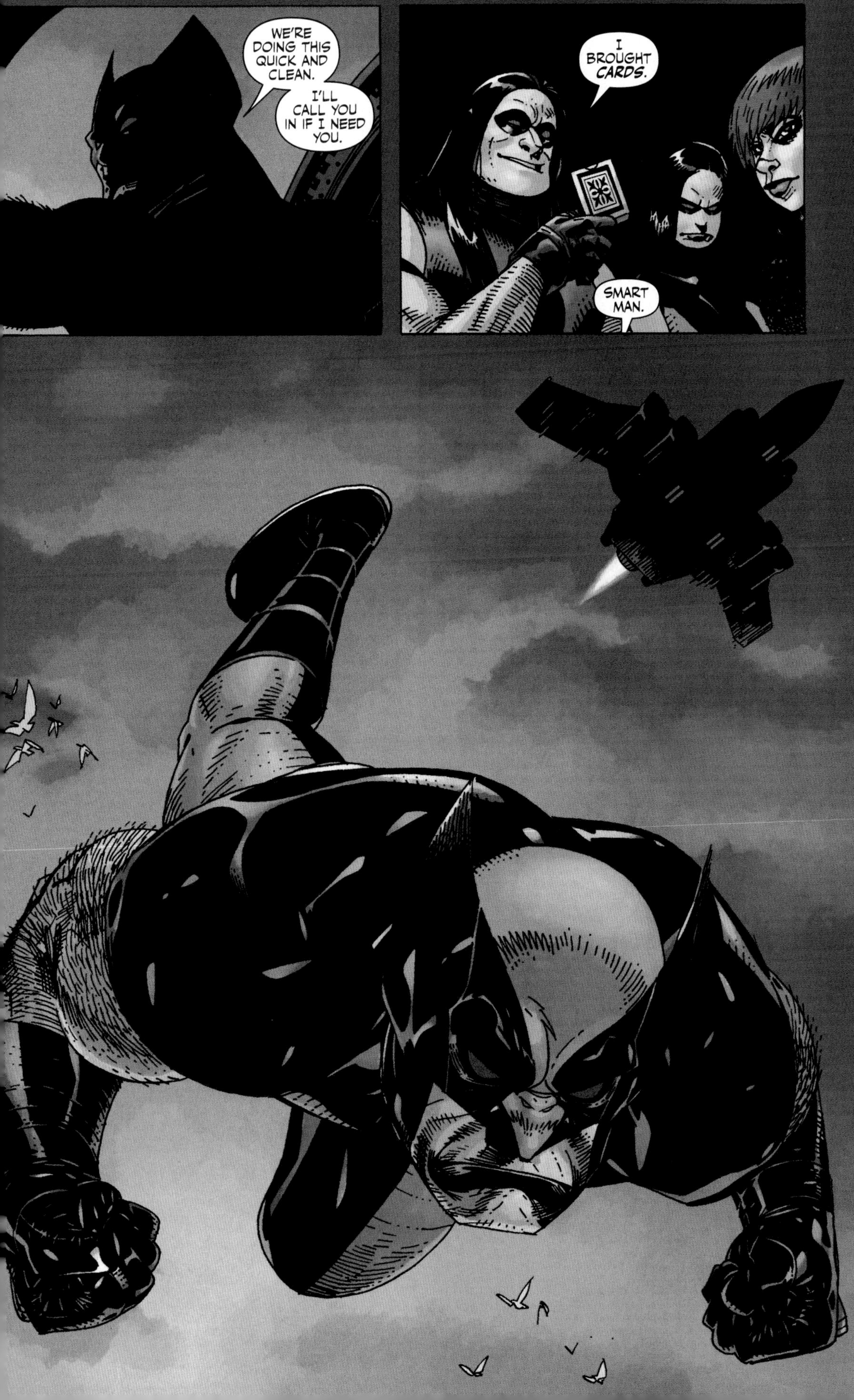

I BROUGHT CARDS.
SMART MAN.

Hydra base 2994.

YOU HEAR SOME-THING?
I HEAR YOU CHEWING YOUR FOOD--WHICH IS EXTREMELY UNPLEASANT, LET ME TELL YOU.

SHUNK!
NOW I *KNOW* I HEARD SOME-THING.
WHAT THE--?!

K-LANKK!

OH, JEEZ--INTRUDER, INTRUDER!
I SEE HIM!
BLAM! BLAM!
KRAK!
WHUDD!
KROOM!
THIS MAN--WHERE IS HE?
S--SECTION SEVENTEEN.

KEEP IT QUICK, KEEP IT CLEAN.

NO KILLING -- NO *CLAWS* UNTIL I FIND THE ONE I'M LOOKING FOR.

SECTION 17

IRK!
FWUMP!

NIGHT NIGHT.

HRM.

SOUND THE ALARM. SECURITY HAS BEEN BREACHED.

HM?
WRAKK!
WROKK!
WHUDD!

KE-RACK
QUICK AND CLEAN... ...SO MUCH FOR THAT..
WRAMM!
OH--OH, JEEZ... AND THERE GOES "NO KILLING".
I HOPE YOU'RE NOT--
PSSSSH
THERE'S BEEN A BREACH, THIS SECTION IS--
BOY, AM I HAPPY TO SEE YOU.

YOU DARE--
WRAMM!
I NEED YOU ALIVE -- NOT AWAKE.
OH GREAT.
RELEASE THE AGENT AND STAND DOWN AT ONCE. WE ARE AUTHORIZED TO USE WHATEVER MEANS NECESSARY TO TAKE YOU DOWN.

RUNNING -- NOT AN OPTION.
DON'T SUPPOSE YOU'D BE WILLING TO GIVE ME A PASS ON THIS ONE?
CHAK!

LAST WARNING.

I KNOW YOU'RE NOT EXACTLY AN ORGANIZATION THAT RECOGNIZES THE IMPORTANCE OF THE INDIVIDUAL...

...BUT YOUR GUNS AREN'T GOING TO DO MUCH TO ME -- AND THIS GUY --

DON'T SHOOT!
HOLD YOUR FIRE!

UNEXPECTED BUT NOT UNWELCOME.
SNIKT

GET HIM!
YOU BOYS ARE IN FOR A WORLD OF HURT!
OH, NO YOU DON'T--!
I'M NOT LEAVING WITHOUT THIS GUY-- I WAS TOLD TO BRING HIM IN AND I AIM TO DO SO.
WRAMM
BUT THEY DIDN'T SAY ANYTHING ABOUT HIM HAVING *BRUISES!*

KEEP IT COMING -- THERE'S MORE THAN ENOUGH OF THIS GUY TO GO AROUND!
YOU'RE DEFINITELY GOING TO FEEL THAT IN THE MORNING.
SERVES YOU RIGHT FOR BEING SO DAMN HEAVY.
CLICK
GOOD THING THEY GOT RID OF THE STAIRS...

11

13

DING
16
SORRY, THIS ELEVATOR IS --

16
BRATTTA TATATA

16
SIT TIGHT, BUB!

DING

COULDA JUST STAYED ON THE ELEVATORS--
--BUT THESE GUYS WERE ASKING FOR IT!

DING!
YOU BETTER BE WORTH IT.
I'LL BE ON THE ROOF IN NINETY SECONDS -- BE THERE.
AND TELL CYCLOPS WE'RE ON OUR WAY.

St. Francis Memorial Hospital, San Francisco.
YOU HAVE ALL MADE A TERRIBLE MISTAKE.
YOU'LL REGRET THIS VERY SOON -- I ASSURE YOU.
YOU'RE HYDRA, CUT OFF ONE LIMB AND TWO GROW BACK IN ITS PLACE. YOU'VE BEEN REPLACED BY NOW -- YOU WON'T BE MISSED.
NICE JOB, WOLVERINE.
CASSANDRA?
WHAT ARE YOU DOING HERE?
WHAT'S GOING ON?

TOD
AUFMAN -- YOU
E A DAUGHTER...
D SHE IS VERY
SICK.
SHE'S CONTRACTED A RARE BLOOD DISEASE AND IF SHE DOESN'T RECEIVE A BONE MARROW TRANSPLANT -- SHE WILL DIE.
WE'VE HACKED INTO HYDRA RECORDS -- YOU ARE A COMPATIBLE DONOR. IF YOUR DAUGHTER DOESN'T GET WHAT SHE NEEDS -- SHE WILL BE DEAD IN A MATTER OF DAYS.
WHY DIDN'T YOU TELL ME?
I DIDN'T WANT YOU TO KNOW -- I DIDN'T WANT MY GIRL TO KNOW HER FATHER IS A MONSTER -- A TERRORIST.
BESIDES, YOU NEVER WOULD HAVE ACCEPTED HER ONCE YOU LEARNED WHAT SHE WAS.
MY DAUGHTER IS A MUTANT.
YOUR DAUGHTER IS FIGHTING FOR HER LIFE.
SHE NEEDS YOUR HELP. WE JUST NEED A SMALL SAMPLE SO WE CAN SYNTHESIZE WHAT WE NEED.
DON'T THINK ABOUT IT TOO HARD, SCUMBAG.
WE TOOK YOU TO THE WELL AND WE CAN SURE AS HELL MAKE YOU DRINK.

THEY'VE TRACKED US SOMEHOW!
THIS IS GOING TO GET UGLY.
STAND DOWN AND RELEASE AGENT KAUFMAN AT ONCE!
NOBODY DO ANYTHING STUPID.
THE ONLY STUPID THING WOULD BE TO TRY AND KEEP ME HERE.

DO YOU HONESTLY THINK ANY OF YOU ARE GOING TO MAKE IT OUT OF THIS ALIVE?

DON'T INSULT MY INTELLIGENCE, WOLVERINE.
I KNOW YOU DON'T WANT A FIGHT HERE--IN THIS ROOM, WITH MY VERY FRAGILE DAUGHTER CLINGING TO LIFE. THERE'S TOO MUCH AT STAKE.

HOW DID THEY FIND YOU SO QUICKLY?
MY BLOOD IS LACED WITH AN ISOTOPE HYDRA CAN USE TO TRACK ME.
WHICH SHOULD PUT TO REST THE QUESTION OF HOW THEY FOUND ME AND MAKE YOU WONDER WHY HYDRA WOULD GO TO ALL THE TROUBLE OF RESCUING LITTLE OLD ME...

...GENERALS DON'T ALWAYS WEAR BIGGER HATS.

NOW, UNLESS YOU WANT TO PUT THIS GIRL AND HER POOR MOTHER IN HARM'S WAY--I SUGGEST YOU ALLOW ME TO BE ON MY WAY.

THE GIRL? YOU'RE JUST GOING TO LET HER DIE?
...
I'M AFRAID I DON'T HAVE THE TIME TO GIVE A PROPER SAMPLE.
YOU'VE GOT ABOUT THREE SECONDS BEFORE I CHANGE MY MIND.

SNIKT!
HEH.
I'M NOT SURE OUR MANTRA WILL APPLY IN THIS CASE...

CASSANDRA,
OUR TIME TOGETHER WAS
WONDERFUL. YOU SHOULD HAVE
TOLD ME ABOUT OUR
DAUGHTER.

I'M
SORRY.

YOU'RE
GOING TO BE
OKAY...

DAMN. THAT'S HARDCORE.
THE END

7

KYOTO, JAPAN.
EVERYTHING YOU ASKED FOR.
WHAT ABOUT SINISTER?
THERE HAS BEEN NO ACTIVITY AT THE TARGET LOCATION FOR WEEKS.
THEY SAY HE IS DEAD.
YEAH, SURE HE IS.
THE BUYER HAS REQUESTED LOT 146, SPECIMEN NUMBER FIVE.
AND WHO'S THE BUYER AGAIN?
GET THE ITEM, THEN CALL THE NUMBER. THAT IS ALL YOU NEED TO KNOW.
I COULD HAVE BROUGHT THIS JOB TO ANY NUMBER OF OPERATIVES. YOU KNOW MY FEE, I--
EH?
NO...
NO!
WHAT ABOUT MY MONEY?!

SAN FRANCISCO.
RRRRING! RRRRING!
HELLO?
HELLO? HELLO?
YOU SHOULD BE SPEAKING NOW, YES?
PHONE, INCREASE VOLUME.
PHONE! I AM TALKING TO YOU!
GIANT
IDIOT MACHINE! I AM TALKING TO YOU!
JIMMY.
WHA--?
Connected...
00:43
X-men HQ (SF)

LET'S GO.
JAMES? JA--
TH!
WHAT DO YOU WANT, LOGAN?
YOU GOIN' ON A TRIP? GOT A VACATION PLANNED?
YOU WERE RIGHT, OKAY?
YOU TOLD ME TO WALK AWAY, AND I DIDN'T LISTEN.

NOW I CAN'T TALK TO MY FRIENDS, I CAN'T TALK TO THE X-MEN, I CAN'T EVEN TALK TO HEPZIBAH.
SO I'M GOING TO TALK TO THE ONE PERSON I CAN.

YOU GOT A PROBLEM WITH THAT?
NO.

TELL YOUR BROTHER I SAID "HI."

'S AERIE, COLORADO.

I KNOW. I KNOW WHAT'S GOING ON HERE.

I'VE SEEN AND HEARD ENOUGH TO FIGURE IT OUT, LAURA.

AND I KNOW THEY'RE KEEPING HE TRUTH FROM THE OTHER X-MEN.
SO I GUESS THE QUESTION IS, WHAT ARE THEY OING TO DO WITH E? I'M NOT GOING O USE MY POWERS TO KILL. AND THEY AN'T JUST KEEP ME HERE, ALANI AND THE OTHERS WILL NOTICE.
THERE IS A 98.2 PERCENT CHANCE YOU WILL TELL SOMEONE WHAT YOU'VE SEEN HERE, GIVEN YOUR AGE AND CURRENT ROMANTIC RELATIONSHIP.
THE ONLY TACTICAL RECOURSE CYCLOPS HAS IS TO KILL YOU.

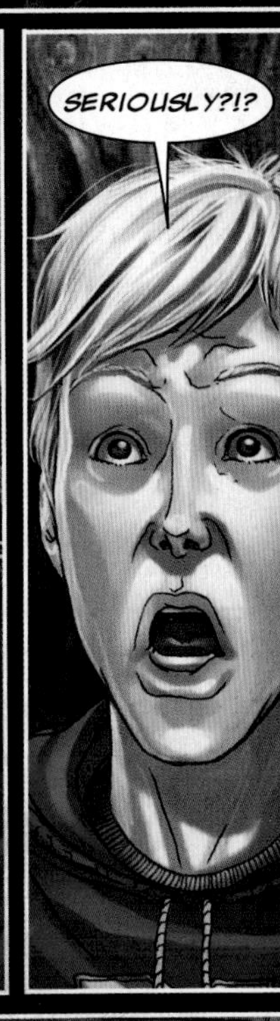

YES. BUT--
COME ON, PUNKS. WE'VE GOT WORK TO DO.

"*BUT*" WHAT?! CYCLOPS SHOULD KILL ME BUT *WHAT*?
LAURA? **LAURA!!**

I MUST WARN YOU...I AM HIGHLY PROFICIENT IN RACQUETBALL.
GOOD FOR YOU.
YOU READY, SLIM?

PLEASE... SCOTT...DON'T DO THIS.
I DON'T WANT TO HURT ANYONE.
WE'RE READY.
LOGAN...

WE GOTTA KNOW, RAHNEY.
COME ON OUT, WARREN.

THERE HAS TO BE A BETTER WAY TO DO THIS.

WE LIKE THE DIRECT APPROACH.
LOOK AT HIM, RAHNE.
NO...LOGAN, PLEASE, I CANNAE!
YOU DON'T KNOW THE EVIL IN ME...

THAT'S WHAT WE'RE TRYING TO FIND OUT, DARLIN'.
LOOK AT HIM!

ANGEL.
SINCLAIR?
GGGRRRRR...
DAMMIT. HERE WE GO.
UHN!!
RRRAAAA!!!

WHAM!
NO!!
GRAAAH!! RRAAA!!
NO... NO...GET BACK...
EVERYONE... GET...
DIE!
FT!
FT!
FT!
FT!
FT!
FT!
TOK!
HSSSS!!
TOK!
TOK!
TOK!
TOK!

MOVE!!
HURRK!

RAAAR!!
HNN! CYKE! HE'S COMING IN!

UHN!!!
ZARK!

SKASH!

HURR!! KILL...THE ANGEL...
TAKE THE WINGS...
RAAA!!!
FOLEY! GET IN HERE!

KILL YOU ALL!!
HANG ON, RAHNE...
JUST DO IT!
EAT YOUR HEARTS--

--UHNNN...
SLEEP.

ELIXIR, GET WOLFSBANE OUT OF HERE.
ARCHANGEL IS COMING BACK.

WHERE IS SHE!?

UFF!

WARREN! LOOK AT ME!
WARREN!
I...AM... DEATH!
THIS ISN'T YOU, WARREN! THIS IS *HIM* TALKING.
SHE TOOK MY *WINGS!* SHE HAS TO *DIE!*
YOU'RE STRONGER THAN HIM, WARREN.
SHE HAS TO... SHE... RAHNE.

ANYONE ELSE WANNA FLIP OUT NOW? CYKE?
SHUT UP, LOGAN.
ARE YOU OKAY, WARREN? ARE YOU GOING TO BE ABLE TO CONTROL THIS?
I...I THINK SO. GOOD LORD, SCOTT...WHAT DID APOCALYPSE DO TO ME?

S.H.I.E.L.D. ADMINISTRATIVE OFFICES, WASHINGTON, DC.
NOK NOK NOK
H.YOUNG DIVISION C
AGENT YOUNG? YOU WANTED TO SEE ME?
PLEASE COME IN, AGENT MORALES. HAVE A SEAT.
I'M SORRY, HAVE ME MET?
NO. THIS OFFICE DEALS WITH UNSOLVED CASES. YOU'VE NEVER HAD ONE.
UNTIL NOW... THE PURIFIER MASSACRE.
THE CASE ISN'T CLOSED YET.
ONE OF YOUR REPORTS RAISED A RED-FLAG IN MY OFFICE. I MAY BE ABLE TO HELP YOU.
APPARENTLY, YOU AND I ARE AFTER THE SAME TARGET.
FOR NICK FURY'S EYES ONLY
FIELD REPORT, CAPTAIN AMERICA
SUBJECT: X-23

Welcome to NEW MEXICO
"The Land of Enchantment"

EVERYONE STILL ALIVE?
LAURA? SUMMERS? WHAT--
WHAT THE HELL?
UHHHHH... GOOD MORNING?
SUMMERS...

SUMMERS!!

IS THIS WHO YOU ARE NOW? YOU BRING IN THE *CUCKOOS* TO MINDWIPE FOLEY? THIS IS EXACTLY THE KIND OF #$!% WE TURNED AWAY FROM XAVIER FOR!
ENEMIES IS ONE THING, PROTECTING THE PUBLIC, FINE, BUT ELIXIR...HE MAY BE A STUPID SNOT-NOSED KID, BUT HE'S ONE OF US!

ARE YOU DONE?
GO TO HELL!

HOW FAR ARE YOU WILLING TO GO? WE'RE CROSSING A LINE, YEAH, BUT HOW LONG UNTIL WE'RE NO DIFFERENT?
HOW LONG UNTIL WE DON'T EVEN SEE THE LINE?

CYCLOPS DIDN'T CALL THE CUCKOOS.

I DID.
TO HELP SAVE RAHNE SINCLAIR.
THE CUCKOOS WON'T TALK. THEY ARE LOYAL TO CYCLOPS OVER EMMA FROST.
SHE CAN READ OUR MINDS INDIVIDUALLY.
BUT TOGETHER...
...WE CAN SHUT HER OUT.
SO WHY ARE THEY JACKING FOLEY?
BECAUSE I ASKED THEM TO.
I DON'T WANT TO KNOW ABOUT THIS. BECAUSE IF I KNOW WHO YOU'RE GOING AFTER, I MAY WANT TO KILL AGAIN, JUST LIKE I DID WITH STRYKER.
AND I DON'T WANT TO BE THAT PERSON.

BUT I DON'T WANT TO STOP YOU FROM DOING WHAT NEEDS TO BE DONE.
WELL, HELL. NOW I WANNA KEEP HIM.
ARE YOU SURE I DIDN'T HAVE THE CUCKOOS PLANT THAT ANSWER INSIDE HIM, LOGAN? SINCE YOU'RE KEEPING US HONEST AND ALL.
WHAT DO YOU WANT, AN APOLOGY?
I HAVEN'T GONE EVIL. I HAVEN'T BEEN TAKEN OVER, I HAVEN'T BEEN REPLACED.
WE'RE ENTERING NEW TERRITORY, AND IT'S DARK.
BUT WE'RE STILL THE GOOD GUYS.
THAT'S GREAT. BECAUSE THE BAD GUYS ARE MAKING THEIR MOVE.

--REPEATING THE TOP STORY, FORMER PRESIDENTIAL CANDIDATE GRAYDON CREED, FORMERLY THOUGHT TO BE THE VICTIM OF AN ASSASSINATION PLOT, IS ALIVE.
WE'RE BRINGING YOU LIVE TO A PRESS CONFERENCE ALREADY IN PROGRESS.
GRAYDON CREED PRESS CONFERENCE
University of Texas Longhorns, wins
--HAD BEEN MARKED FOR DEATH BY MUTANT TERRORISTS.
WITH THE COOPERATION OF THE U.S. GOVERNMENT AND S.H.I.E.L.D., I AND SEVERAL OTHER HIGH-RISK TARGETS WERE PUT INTO PROTECTIVE CUSTODY, AND REPLACED WITH S.H.I.E.L.D. DECOYS.
BUT WE CANNOT HIDE ANY MORE.
WE COULD NOT SIT BY AND WATCH AS MANKIND IGNORES THE GREATEST THREAT THAT WE'VE EVER KNOWN.
THIS IS BAD, RIGHT?

"MANY PEOPLE BELIEVE THE DANGER POSED BY MUTANTS IS A THING OF THE PAST, BUT IT IS NOT.
"THEY BELIEVE THAT BECAUSE MUTANTS HAVE GONE INTO HIDING, THAT WE ARE SAFE. WE ARE NOT.
THE QUESTION IS OT IF THEY WILL TRIKE AGAIN, BUT WHEN.
"AND WE MUST BE READY.
"GENOSHA DESTROYED? 16 MILLION MUTANTS DEAD?
"IT TAKES ONLY ONE MUTANT TO KILL MILLIONS OF HUMANS.
"THE MUTANTS HAVE BEEN CONFINED TO A GOVERNMENT CAMP?
"THINK AGAIN. THEY WALK AMONG US.

"THEY DON'T WANT YOU TO KNOW THAT MAGNETO IS ALIVE AND ON THE LOOSE.
"THEY DON'T WANT YOU TO KNOW THAT MUTANT TERRORISTS ARE CREATING TRAINING CAMPS RIGHT HERE IN THE UNITED STATES.
"THEY DON'T WANT YOU TO KNOW THAT A NEW WAR IS COMING."
MANKIND MUST DEFEND ITSELF.
WE MUST BE READY.
AND IF HUMANITY IS TO SURVIVE...
AND IF HUMANITY IS TO SURVIVE... I WILL NEED ALL OF YOUR HELP.

BZZZT BZZZT
YEAH, FOLEY. IT'S BAD.
REAL FLAMIN' BAD.
IF BASTION IS PUTTING CREED BACK IN WASHINGTON, WE'VE GOT TO ASSUME HE'S PUTTING THE OTHERS BACK IN PLACE.
THAT MEANS TRASK AND LANG IN THE D.O.D.
THAT MEANS SENTINELS.
GREAT.
SO? WHO DO WE GO AFTER FIRST?
NONE OF THEM. WE'VE GOT A NEW TARGET.
THE VANISHER.
COME AGAIN?

"IT'S NOT *HIM* WE'RE AFTER, LOGAN...

"...IT'S WHAT HE'S *TAKEN.*"

PSSH!

PSSH!

WELL, THAT WAS EASY.
LEGACY VIRUS

8

THE AMERICAN SOUTHWEST. NIGHT.
WHAT HAVE I BECOME? MY SWEETEST FRIEND...

EVERYONE I KNOW GOES AWAY IN THE END...

YOU COULD HAVE IT ALL... MY EMPIRE OF DIRT...

I WILL LET YOU DOWN... I WILL MAKE YOU--

SHNK!
KSSSHH!
CLANK!
CHOOM!!

TOKYO, JAPAN.
A MUTANT NAMED SCALPHUNTER CONTACTED CYCLOPS ABOUT THE THEFT.
HE HAD CONNECTIONS WITH SINISTER RIGHT UP UNTIL HE DIED, AND WHEN ONE OF SINISTER'S LABS WAS BROKEN INTO, HE WAS THE FIRST TO KNOW ABOUT IT.
COMICTORAN
SCALPHUNTER ALSO KNEW EXACTLY WHAT HAD BEEN TAKEN, AND IT SCARED HIM.
THIS IS A MISTAKE.
WE'RE DOWN TWO MEN. WE NEED HIM WITH US.
VANISHER STOLE A TARGETED VIRUS DESIGNED FOR ONE PURPOSE...TO KILL MUTANTS.
WORTHINGTON CANNOT BE TRUSTED.
BUT INSTEAD O TELLING THE RE OF SINISTER'S LO LIFE FOLLOWE WHAT HAPPENE SCALPHUNTER TURNED TO US FOR HELP
YOU'VE MENTIONED THAT ABOUT FIFTY FLAMIN' TIMES ALREADY, LAURA! I GET IT. YOU DON'T LIKE THE PLAN.
BUT SCALPHUNTER IS A MARAUDER. A MARAUDER PUT TWO SPIKES THROUGH MY WINGS.
SINCLAIR IS BACK AT T BASE. WORTHINGTO NEEDS TO--
HE SHOULDN'T COME LOOKING FOR MY HELP WHEN HE'S SCARED... HE SHOULD BE SCARED OF ME.
›YAMAE‹
WE'RE ON.
Mister Donut

COTT ASKED ME IF I
WAS OKAY...IF I FELT
KE I COULD HANDLE
MISSION SO SOON
TER... "THE ATTACK."
TOLD HIM
WAS FINE.
I LIED.
SCOTT NEEDED ME TO GO WITH WOLVERINE BECAUSE I'VE GOT A HISTORY WITH THE MAN WHO BROKE INTO SINISTER'S LAB.
I KNOW THE VANISHER.
BUT THE VANISHER DOESN'T KNOW ME. NOT ANYMORE.
TELFORD...
WORTHINGTON?! WHAT THE HELL ARE YOU DOING HERE?
YOU KNOW WHAT I'M HERE FOR, TELFORD. GIVE ME THE VIRUS.
NOW.
I WANT HIM TO RUN. TO FIGHT.
EVERY FIBER OF MY BEING SCREAMS FOR ME TO REACH OUT AND TAKE OFF HIS HEAD.

I DON'T KNOW WHAT YOU'RE TALKING ABOUT.
THIS ISN'T A GAME, VANISHER. YOU'RE IN WAY OVER YOUR HEAD, AND THIS IS YOUR ONLY CHANCE.
GIVE ME THE VIRUS... OR ELSE.
NO. MAKE ME TAKE IT FROM YOU.
UHN!
SMAK
OR WHAT, PRETTY BOY? YOU'LL WING ME?
LAST TIME WE MET, YOU COST ME A FORTUNE. AND IF YOU TOUCH ME AGAIN, I'LL TELEPORT YOUR ARM OFF.
PERFECT.
I KNEW I COULD COUNT ON HIM.
NOW I CAN FINALLY STOP PRETENDING.
NOW I GET TO DO WHAT I CAME HERE FOR.
NOT A DAMN WORD LAURA!
COVER WARREN, MAKE SURE HE DOESN'T KILL ANYONE. I'LL GRAB VANISHER.

AAAHH!!
STUPID PRETTY BOY RICH KID...
RRRAAAA!!
GAH!
BLAM!!
KTANG!!
UHHHN!
SNIPER. 10TH STORY. I WILL--
KMVT!
HTT!
STAY! I'VE GOT THIS.
WHOOOOSH!
HNN!!
CRACK!

WHAT THE HELL-- LAURA...
VANISHER ESCAPED.
WHAT?! DAMMIT!!
I'VE GOT THE SCENT OF THE SHOOTER'S RIFLE. ARCHANGEL IS IN PURSUIT.
ARCHANGEL, COME IN.
ARCHANGEL, THE TARGET IS MOVING!
I LOSE MYSELF.
MY MIND IS CONSUMED WITH KILLING...
ARCHANGEL IS NOT RESPONDIN WE SHOULD NO HAVE--
OKAY, ALREADY! I GET IT!
KILLING FOR HIM.
MY MISSION...MY ONLY PURPOSE... TO FIND THOSE FIT TO SURVIVE.
I AM THE BRINGER OF THE APOCALYPSE... I AM THE CRUCIBLE.
CRASH!!
HSSS!! YOU'RE DEAD DO YOU HEAR ME?!

I HEAR YOU.
THE QUESTION IS, DO YOU HEAR ME?
CHA-CHAK!
OM-N-O?
HI.
AND THEN, SOMETIMES, I REMEMBER MYSELF.

COLORADO.
NIGHT.
MOIRA, I NEED YOU...
DANI... SOMEBODY... PLEASE...HELP ME...
RRAAARRRR!!
PLEASE... GOD. PLEASE!!!!
GOD... PLEASE FORGIVE ME...
AAAAHH!

HHNNN...
...THE HELL... WAS...
CHOK
I'M COMING FOR YOU, GOTAL.

...ONE MORE TIME, DOMINO. WHY DID YOU SHOOT ME IN THE HEAD?
YOU PUT YOUR HEAD IN BETWEEN ME AND PORTER. NOT MY FAULT.

AND YOU WERE WEARING THAT FANCY NEW COSTUME. I COULDN'T EVEN TELL IT WAS YOU.

YOU ARE BOTH BREAKING RADIO SILENCE.
WE'RE NOT GOING TO LET A LITTLE THING LIKE A HEAD WOUND GET IN THE WAY OF A GOOD TIME, ARE WE, LOGAN? BY THE WAY, THE GOLD KID LOOKS NERVOUS.
DON'T SCREW THIS UP, FOLEY.

WOW, THAT WAS MOTIVATIONAL.
I TOLD HIM I DIDN'T WANT TO DO THIS.
YOU'D BETTER BE RIGHT ABOUT THIS, DOM.
HEY, IT'S ME. I'VE BEEN ON THE VANISHER'S CASE FOR A WEEK. I KNOW HIS ROUTINE.

VT!
SNIKT!!
WHA--?
RRAAA!
AIIEEE!!
VT!

HE JUST JUMPED FROM SAFEHOUSE TWO. GET READY FOR INCOMING.
TELFORD...
VT!
WORTH-- WORTHINGTON?
NOT WORTHINGTON.
DEATH!!
GAAA-
VT!

VT!
--AAHH!!
HUP!
NUUGH!!
VT!

I'M SORRY.
AAAH!!
I... I... I'M OKAY? OH, GOD...
WHAT DID YOU DO TO ME?
I KILLED YOU.
WHAT ARE YOU TALKING ABOUT? WHO ARE YOU?
HIS NAME IS ELIXIR AND HE'S TELLING THE TRUTH. WE JUST KILLED YOU.
BUUUUT... YOU MAY WANT TO GET A SECOND OPINION ON THAT.
VT!
THAT WAS FUN.

DOCTOR? ISHA?
SO, UH... EVERYTHING OKAY? I FEEL OKAY.
DOES SOMEONE WANT TO TALK TO ME?
I'M RIGHT HERE!
HEY!!
SHOULD I BE WORRIED?!

...AND THAT'S THE STORY WITH THE PUNISHER.
SO. YOU'VE FORMED YOUR OWN LITTLE KILL CREW. FINALLY!
IT'S COMPLICATED.
WHY IS THE GIRL STANDING LIKE THAT?
SHE LIKES TO BE PREPARED.
WOLVERINE SAYS WE CAN TRUST DOMINO. I FIND MYSELF NOT CARING. THE OTHERS SHOULD KNOW ABOUT X-FORCE. THE WORLD SHOULD KNOW THAT MUTANTKIND WILL RULE--
OH, GOD.
I CAN'T GET IT OUT OF MY HEAD. SCOTT KNOWS... HE'S BEEN THERE. BUT WHA IF I CAN'T CONTROL IT?
SO WHAT, SHE'S A BOY SCOUT?
HOW LONG CAN I KEEP UP THE ACT? I LOOK AT THE OTHERS, AND WANT TO SEE...GOD HELP ME, I LOOK AT THEM AND WANT TO KILL THEM.
TO SEE IF THEY'RE STRONG ENOUGH.
YOU SHOULD NOT HAVE MISSED YOUR SHOT. YOUR POWERS SHOULD HAVE INSURED A KILL.
YOU'RE A CREEPY LITTLE GIRL, HAS ANYONE EVER TOLD YOU THAT?
WHAT IF WE'RE WRONG? WHAT IF HE DOESN'T COME BACK?
I HAVE TO SMILE FOR THE OTHER X-MEN. I HAVE TO MAKE JOKES. I HAVE TO BE WARREN.
WHAT THE HELL DID YOU DO TO ME?!
I AM WARREN.
VT!
BUT I COULD KILL THIS ONE.

WHAT THE HELL IS THIS?!
WHAM!!
HEH. LOOKS LIKE A TUMOR. NASTY ONE, TOO.

NICE JOB WORKING IN THE TEAM LOGO.

THANKS! I THOUGHT ABOUT MAKING IT A HAPPY FACE AT FIRST BUT I DIDN'T KNOW HOW LONG I HAD...

...PLUS THE FACT THAT I NEEDED TO MAKE SURE IT--
DON'T RUIN IT, FOLEY.

AAAHH!
LISTEN UP, BUB!

YOU'VE GOT AN INOPERABLE BRAIN TUMOR. YOU'RE GONNA DIE UNLESS YOU HELP US.
THE ONLY CHOICE YOU HAVE TO MAKE...

...IS HOW BAD WE HURT YOU BEFORE YOU DO.
NOW WHERE IS THE $@%*ING VIRUS?!

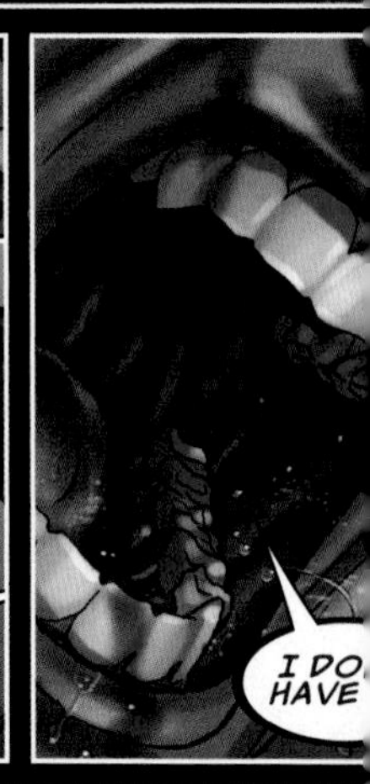
I DO
HAVE

WRONG ANSWER, BUB.

ARIZONA.
APPROACHING THE CAMP VERDE BURIAL SITE.
BRING IT ON, YOU SON OF A $%&#.

RRRROOOAARR!

X-FORCE

CHOI
OBACK

9

THE VANISHER'S SAFEHOUSE, JAPAN.
AAAHHHH!!
SNIKT!!
WRONG ANSWER, BUB.
TRY AGAIN.
GAAAHH!!
OHMIGOD... WHY DID YOU DO THAT?!
LET ME--
NO. NOT YET.
WHAT THE HELL IS WRONG WITH YOU?!
I'M TELLING YOU THE TRUTH! I DON'T HAVE THE VIRUS!
THEN WHO DOES?!
IF I TELL YOU, YOU'LL THINK I'M CRAZY OR LYING!
TRY ME.
SINISTER'S LAB. EARLIER.
LEGACY VIRUS
"ALRIGHT! ALRIGHT... WHEN I GOT TO THE LAB EVERYTHING WAS GOING FINE BUT--"
WELL, THAT WAS EASY.
GRRRRRR...
EH?
"WHO HAS IT?!"

IE MARAUDERS.
"SABRETOOTH, HARPOON, VERTIGO, SCRAMBLER... THERE WERE OTHERS, TOO, I COULDN'T MAKE THEM OUT.
RRRAAAA!!!
"I-I DON'T KNOW WHERE THEY CAME FROM OR HOW THEY FOUND ME...BUT THEY WERE OUT FOR BLOOD... MY BLOOD."
AAAAAHHH!
HURRR... HURRR...
"SO I VANISHED.
"AND, UH... DROPPED THE VIAL."
VT!

SURE, WHY THE HELL NOT? EVERYONE ELSE IS COMING BACK FROM THE DEAD, WHY NOT SABRETOOTH?
IT'S NOT LIKE I CUT OFF HIS HEAD OR ANYTHING.
NO...IT'S NOT SABRETOOTH. IT'S A CLONE.
I NEVER THOUGHT I'D SEE THE DAY WHEN THE X-MEN SLICE OPEN A GUY'S NOSE TO MAKE HIM TALK.
MY NAME IS DOMINO, AND APPARENTLY I'VE MISSED A FEW MEETINGS.
WE'VE SEEN THIS BEFORE WITH SINISTER, REMEMBER?
HE'S GOT CLONE FARMS OF THE MARAUDERS... AFTER HE DIED, THEY MUST HAVE HATCHED OR SOMETHING.
THEY'RE NOT REAL.
LOGAN SAID HE'D FILL ME IN LATER, BUT THE ONE THING HE COULD TELL ME...
...MADE ME PRETTY HAPPY.
FINE. HERE'S HOW IT IS.
CRYBABY HERE TELEPORTS US IN. WE GET THE VIRUS. WE DESTROY IT, AND ANYTHING ELSE WE FIND IN THERE.
WE BURN IT ALL RIGHT TO THE DAMN GROUND.
WAIT... TELEPORT? YOU'RE NOT TALKING ABOUT ME, ARE YOU?

TSIDE CAMP VERDE,
ZONA.
WHAM!!
RRAAAA...
???
FWMP!
WHAT THE HELL--?
GRRRRRR...
OHHHHH, SH--

--!!!!!!!!!
AARGHH!!
CRACK!
HUUK... HUHN...
OKAY... OKAY...I CAN'T TOUCH IT...BUT IT CAN TOUCH ME...
THAT'S NOT GOOD...
ROOAAARRR!

NINETY-SEVEN MILES AWAY.
VRROOOMM!!
ROOAAARRR!
SCREEEEEEEECH!
ROOARR...

ANGEL'S AERIE, COLORADO.
...WOLF SIGHTINGS REPORTED BY SEVERAL ROCKY MOUNTAIN RESIDENTS. REMEMBER, IF YOU SEE A WOLF OR ANY OTHER WILD ANIMAL, CALL ANIMAL CONTROL.
NOW, OVER TO WEATHER...
...WHERE THIS COLD SNAP JUST WON'T LET UP!
WEAT
THAT'S RIGHT, KATE, EVEN FOR THE ROCKY MOUNTAIN AREA, THIS HAS BEEN AN UNUSUALLY STRONG AND SUDDEN WINTER STORM.
WE'VE HAD OVER FOUR FEET OF SNOW IN SOME AREAS OVERNIGHT, AND IT DOESN'T LOOK LIKE IT'S LETTING UP ANYTIME SOON.
WE'RE SEEING RECORD LOW TEMPERATURES IN THE HIGHER ALTITUDES, AND HEAVY ICE HAS BEEN REPORTED ON SEVERAL MOUNTAIN ROADS, SO GET THOSE CHAINS ON YOUR TIRES!
THANKS, JIM! IN NATIONAL NEWS, CLEANUP IN THE AFTERMATH OF THE INVASION CONTINUES...

ABERDEEN F.C.
CRKCRKCRK
???
WHAT IN THE WORLD...
GASP!!

THE KITAKYUSHU SMELTING PLANT, JAPAN:

X-FORCE ALWAYS WENT AFTER THE BAD GUYS. WE WERE PROACTIVE, THAT WAS OUR THING. THAT'S WHAT WE DID.

BUT THE SAFETY IS OFF NOW, LOGAN TELLS ME. WE DON'T HOLD BACK.

VT!

FINE! NOW YOU'RE ON YOUR OWN.

I DIDN'T ASK QUESTIONS. I SAW THE WAY ARCHANGEL CAME AFTER ME IN TOKYO... HE WAS PLAYING FOR KEEPS.

THIS DOESN'T LOOK LIKE A LAB, DEAD MAN.

ELIXIR, HE'S A SCARED KID...BUT HE'S NOT SCARED FOR HIMSELF. THE GIRL, YOU CAN SEE IT IN HER EYES. SHE'S A KILLER.

WHAT IS THIS PLACE, PORTER?

SOME FACTORY, I DON'T KNOW. THEY GAVE ME THE BLUEPRINTS, NOT A LECTURE ON HOW MISTER SINISTER PICKS HIS REAL ESTATE.

THE LAB IS IN THE CENTER OF THE COMPLEX.

AND LOGAN... WELL, HE'S LOGAN.

YOU CAN GO FIRST.

UHN!!

I DON'T THINK PROFESSOR XAVIER WOULD APPROVE OF THIS!

TELL ME ABOUT IT.

UP IS DOWN. BLACK IS WHITE. SOMETHING TELLS ME I SHOULD BE WORRIED...

...BUT THEN AGAIN, I'VE GOT LUCK ON MY SIDE.

STILL, I HAVE TO SAY, THIS IS THE GRIMMEST BUNCH OF MUTANTS I'VE EVER SEEN. EVEN CABLE SMILED MORE THAN THESE GUYS.
I SHOULDN'T BE HERE...I TOLD HIM THAT I DIDN'T WANT TO COME...
DON'T WORRY, KIDDO. I'M SURE EVERYTHING WILL BE FINE.
SO...WHO THINKS WE'RE ALL ABOUT TO DIE? I ONLY MENTION IT BECAUSE VANISHER DID SAY HE DROPPED THE VIAL WITH THE VIRUS IN IT. WHAT IF IT BROKE?
THEN WE'RE ALL ABOUT TO HAVE A BAD DAY.
SNFF
HOW MANY?
14 TARGETS... BUT IDENTICAL SCENTS ARE PRESENT. THERE COULD BE MORE.
GREAT. DOM...OPEN IT UP.
LOGAN, YOU SAY THE MOST ROMANTIC THINGS TO ME.
YOU KNOW WHAT I LOVE ABOUT WOLVERINE?
PAF!
BOOOM!
HE REALLY KNOWS HOW TO RELEASE TENSION.
ANY INSPIRATIONAL WORDS?
SURE.
SNIKT!
SNIKT!

IF YOU DIE, TAKE ONE OF THEM WITH YOU.

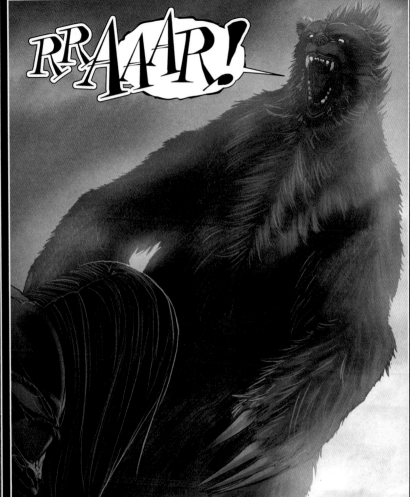

ARIZONA.
ALRIGHT... HNN...ALRIGHT... YOU MANGY... PIECE OF... CRAP...
IF THIS IS...IF THIS IS HOW I DIE...

RRAAAR!

THEN I DIE LIKE AN APACHE.

I DIE A PROUDSTAR!!

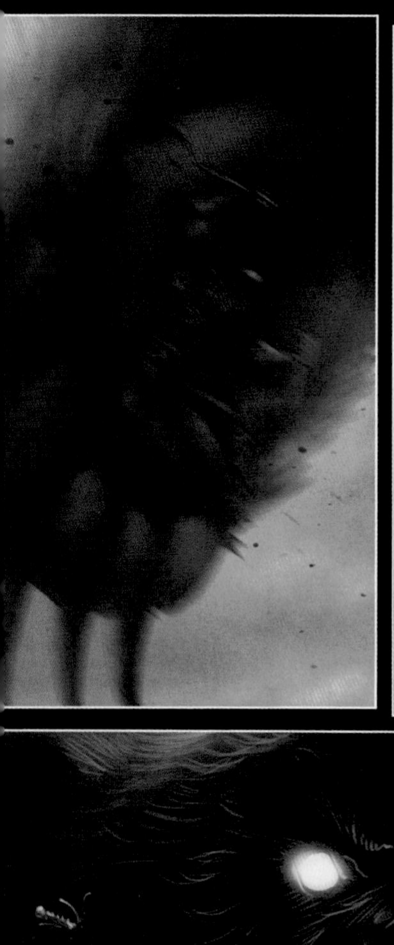

THOOM!
UUHNN!

AAARGHHH!!

GRAAH!

HHHRRRR...

RRAAAAA--
VRROOOMM!!

SHRACKKK!!
ARROOOOO!
RRAAA!!
SHOOOOM!!

TNK! TNK!

IT'S EASY TO FORGET JUST HOW DEADLY MUTANTS CAN BE. ESPECIALLY WHEN WE DRESS IN COLORFUL COSTUMES AND PLAY HERO ALL THE TIME.

AAIIIIEEE--

AS MUCH AS I LIKE LOGAN, I ALWAYS MAKE SURE MY GUNS ARE LOADED WHEN WE HANG OUT.

BUDDABUDDABUDDABUDDA!!

AND ANGEL...HE'S SO GOOD LOOKING, SO CHARMING, THAT WHEN HE BECOMES THIS...WHEN HE BECOMES ***DEATH***, YOU'RE NOT READY FOR IT.

HUK!!

UHN!!

BUT WOLVERINE IS ONE OF THE MOST DANGEROUS MEN ON THE PLANET. HE CAN BE AN X-MAN IN ONE MOMENT AND A SAVAGE BEAST THE NEXT.

CHNK!!

HE'S SOMEHOW BEAUTIFUL AND HORRIBLE AT THE SAME TIME.

ARRGHH!!

GAAIII--
I'M JUST GLAD WE'RE ALL ON THE SAME TEAM.

OH, GOD.
WHAT ARE YOU DOING, KID?! GET IN THERE! WITH YOUR POWER, YOU SHOULD BE TEARING THESE %#& *$ UP!
BLAM! BLAM!
I... I DON'T WANT TO HURT ANYONE...
ARE YOU %*@$ING KIDDING ME? YOU GAVE ME A %*^@ING TUMOR!
I DIDN'T WANT TO DO THAT TO YOU.
WHATEVER, MOTHER TERESA.
LOOK, YOU HEARD WHAT BIRD-BOY SAID, THEY'RE CLONES! THEY'RE NOT REAL!!
ELIXIR!
VANISHER IS RIGHT! DO NOT HOLD BACK!

S.H.I.E.L.D. DIVISION 'C'.
THIS GIRL IS NOT HUMAN.
S.H.I.E.L.D. HAD BEEN AFTER HER FOR SOME TIME UNTIL THE CASE WENT COLD...
GOOD GOD. SHE'S BEEN KILLING PEOPLE SINCE SHE WAS NINE YEARS OLD.
"AGENT MORALES... X-23 HAS KILLED POLITICIANS, DICTATORS, DRUG LORDS, MOB BOSSES, MEMBERS OF AIM, HYDRA AND S.H.I.E.L.D....
"...AND THOSE ARE JUST THE TARGETS THAT WE'VE BEEN ABLE TO IDENTIFY. THERE'S NO TELLING HOW MANY OTHERS SHE'S KILLED.
"SHE'S WANTED IN OVER A DOZEN COUNTRIES AND HAS TIES WITH RADICAL GROUPS THAT ARE...
"...TROUBLING."
AND THE ONLY KNOWN PERSON WITH FIRSTHAND KNOWLEDGE OF THE TARGET...
...IS DEAD. SORRY TO DISAPPOINT YOU, AGENT YOUNG...
...BUT WE'VE GOT NOTHING, UNTIL SHE MAKES ANOTHER MOVE.

HNN... NO...JOHN... PLEASE...

NO!!

WHA--? I'M...I'M ALIVE. I'M ALIVE!!

WHY AM I ALIVE?

BECAUSE YOU HAVE NOT TASTED VENGEANCE... YET.

OKAY, SCRATCH THAT. WHY AM I IN HELL?

YOU KNOW NOTHING OF HELL, MUTANT.

NOW GATHER YOUR STRENGTH...

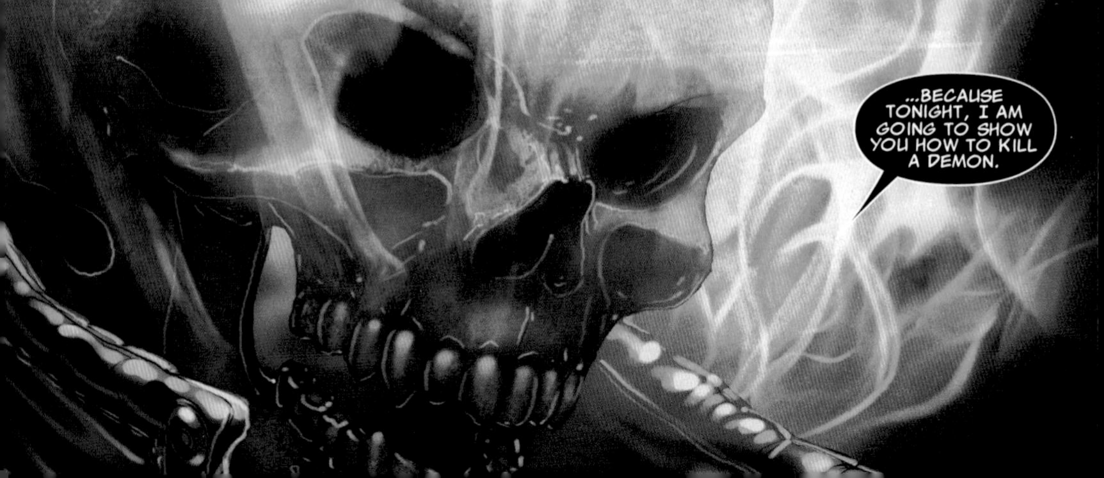

JAPAN.
AND IN THE MIDDLE OF ALL THE MURDER, CHAOS AND BLOOD...
...IS THE VIRUS. HARD TO BELIEVE THAT ONE TINY DROP OF THAT COULD MAKE MUTANTS EXTINCT.
THE VIAL...
GRAAAA!!
I'M CLOSEST TO IT. LUCKY ME.
BLAM! BLAM! BLAM!
GOT IT!! LET'S GET OUT OF--
KA-BOOM!

TAKE THE VIRUS!
EVER SINCE I HOOKED UP WITH THE X-MEN, I'VE HELD BACK. X-MEN DON'T KILL. IT DIDN'T MAKE A LOT OF SENSE TO ME, BUT I RESPECTED IT.
AND NOW, FINALLY, WHEN MUTANTS ARE UP AGAINST THE WALL AS A SPECIES AND IT'S KILL OR BE KILLED...

NO ONE GETS OUT ALIVE!
...THAT'S WHEN MY LUCK RUNS OUT. GREAT.

CHOI
OBACK
10

SEVEN MILES OUTSIDE CAMP VERDE.
THE NATIVES OF THESE LANDS WERE AMONG THE FIRST TO WALK WITHIN THE SPIRIT PLANE. THE WORLD OF THE DEAD AND THAT OF THE LIVING WERE A SINGLE SHARED EXISTENCE.
YOUR PEOPLE HAVE LONG KNOWN ABOUT THE THREAT WE FACE NOW, JAMES PROUDSTAR. BUT FOR ALL YOUR POWER, YOU MAY AS WELL TRY TO KILL THE WIND.
YOUR BLOOD AND YOUR BIRTHRIGHT CONNECT YOU TO THESE FORCES. HOWEVER, YOU ARE NO SHAMAN AND DO NOT KNOW HOW TO ACCESS YOUR ABILITIES.
I WILL SHOW YOU THE PATH LOST BY THE DEATHS OF YOUR ANCESTORS. I WILL OPEN YOU UP TO THE SPIRIT PLANE AND GIVE YOU THE TOOLS NEEDED TO TOUCH THE DEAD, JUST AS THEY HAVE TOUCHED YOU.
THIS DEMON BEAR, HE REEKS OF DARKNESS. BLACK MAGIC SO THICK, EVEN I DO NOT TRULY UNDERSTAND IT.
BUT WE CAN STILL KILL IT. YOU WILL BECOME THE KILLER OF ENEMIES. THE MONSTER SLAYER. OTHER TRIBES HAD A NAME FOR THIS. IT WAS THEIR RELIGION.
THE GHOST DANCE.
MY NAME IS JAMES PROUDSTAR. I AM APACHE, I AM A MUTANT...AND UNTIL RECENTLY I WAS AN X-MAN.
I HAVE NOT LED AN ORDINARY LIFE.

JAPAN. NOW.
UDDABUDDABUDDABUDDABUDDA

VANISHER! GET US OUT, NOW!!

SURE THING.
VT!
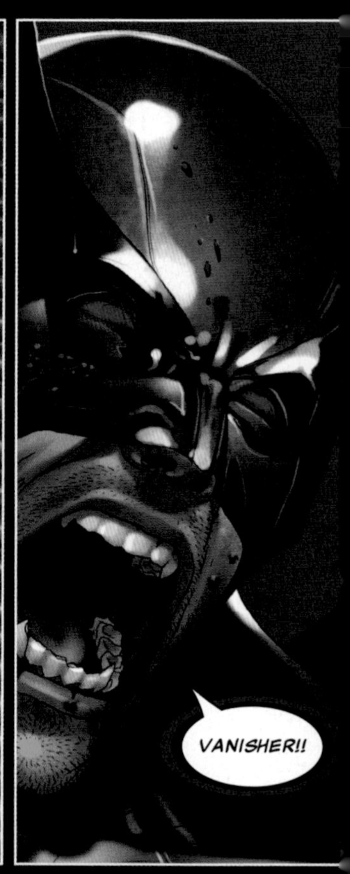
VANISHER!!

I'M GONNA KILL HIM...
WE NEVER SHOULD HAVE--
SHUT UP!!

TNK!
AAAAAHH!!
TNK!
TNK!
TNK!
THE RIGHT... THIS IS THE RIGHT...
HODGE IS MINE.

HEY, DO YOU GUYS WANT TO FOCUS HERE? NOT ALL OF US CAN GET SHOT AND THEN CRAP OUT THE BULLE--
UHN!

I'VE GOT VISUAL ON THE PRIZE.
SNIKT!
LET'S KILL THIS GENE-TRASH AND GET OUT OF--
SHUNK!!
--HEAAARGH!!
AAAHHH!!
LAURA, BEHIND YOU!!

REEEE
HUUH!
REEEEEEE
CRK!
WHAT THE HELL JUST HAPPENED?
OH, GOD. THE VIRUS.
IT'S... IT'S...
IT'S INSIDE HER.

I'VE DEALT WITH DEMON BEARS BEFORE, BUT NEVER LIKE THIS.
ROAR!
NOW YOU WALK IN THE SPIRIT PLANE AND CAN SEE THE BEAST AS IT TRULY IS...
ARE YOU READY, APACHE?
I HAVE NO CONNECTION TO THIS CREATURE...
BUT I'M ABOUT TO.
HELL, YEAH.

GHOST RIDER SMELLS LIKE BURNING FLESH AND I CAN FEEL THE HEAT OF HIS FLAMES INSIDE OF ME. IT'S DISTURBING.
WHAT'S MORE DISTURBING...IS THAT I'M GLAD HE'S HERE.
I DON'T TRUCK WITH MAGIC. NEVER LIKED IT.
SHOW ME WHAT TO HIT, GIVE ME SOMETHING I CAN BURY A KNIFE IN. THAT, I CAN DO.
ARROOO!!
HUH, I
WORKE

ARGHH!!!

UHN!!

DAMN, THIS THING IS ***FAST*** FOR BEING SO BIG.

AYBE IT'S COME TO UNISH ME FOR ALL THE BLOOD ON MY HANDS.

AYBE TODAY IS A GOOD DAY TO DIE.

HNF!!

IT IS IN PAIN. CAN YOU FEEL IT?
PROUDSTAR. LOOK.
WHAT THE @#$% ARE YOU--
WHAT THE HELL IS THAT THING?!
A DEMON BLADE.
THE CREATURE HAS BEEN WOUNDED AND POISONED BY DARK MAGIC.
OKAY, FINE! YOU WANT TO DO SOMETHING NOW?!

HURRRK!
KAFF!
LAURA... LAURA!! HANG ON!
NO, OUR MISSION IS TO DESTROY THE VIRUS.

KILL THE GIRL! WE'LL TAKE THE BODY BACK TO HODGE.
SOMEBODY @#$%ING GET TO LAURA!!
SHOOT HER!
BUDDABUDDABUDDA!
LAURA, WAIT! LAUR--
TAK! TAK!
AAAHHH!
LAURAAAA!!

ROOOARRR!
THE BLADE IS COLD TO THE TOUCH. FOR AN INSTANT, I CONSIDER DRIVING IT IN FURTHER, TO KILL THE BEAST.

RRAAA!!
I GOT IT... I--
PROUDSTAR... SEE WHAT YOU HAVE DONE.
BUT THAT'S NOT WHO I AM. I DON'T WANT TO BE A KILLER.
ARROOOO!!
THIS WAS NO DEMON...
THESE ARE SPIRIT GUIDES. THEY ARE YOUR GODS.
THE KNIFE CORRUPTED THEM, DRIVING THEM MAD WITH OLD MAGIC. THEY LASHED OUT...
SOMEONE *DID* THIS TO THEM? WAIT. WHAT IS IT DOING? WHAT--

HEAR US, APACHE SON.
FEEL OUR PAIN.
WITNESS OUR SUFFERING.
JOHNNY...
AND SEE THE FACE OF OUR ENEMY.

LAURA, STOP!!
WHAT ARE YOU DOING?!
I AM GOING TO DESTROY THE VIRUS.
HOW? BY KILLING YOURSELF?
YES.

NO!!

...CAUGHT... YOU...
NO! YOU'RE RISKING THE LIVES OF EVERY MUTANT ON THE PLANET! LET ME GO!
WHAT ABOUT YOUR LIFE, LAURA?!

IF YOU DO NOT LET GO, I WILL CUT OFF YOUR ARM.
LET ME GO, JOSH.
NO! I WON'T LET YOU DIE.
SNIKT!

LAURA, I KNOW WHY YOU'RE DOING THIS... BUT I DON'T CARE WHAT THEY SAID, CLONE OR NOT, YOU'RE REAL.
LISTEN TO ME. I--I DIDN'T WANT TO BE INVOLVED IN THIS, I DIDN'T WANT TO KNOW, OR EVEN COME. BUT NOW I KNOW WHY I'M HERE. TO SAVE YOU.
I WILL NEVER LET ANOTHER FRIEND OF MINE DIE AGAIN. PLEASE, LAURA...

...LET ME TRY.

I CAN FEEL IT...THE VIRUS...IT'S NOT THE ORIGINAL... GOD, IT'S WORSE IN SOME WAYS...
YOUR SYSTEM IS FIGHTING IT, LAURA...I CAN HELP... WE CAN BURN IT OUT...
I...IT'S GONE. JOSH, YOU DID--
JOSH?
USED TOO MUCH... POWER...
LAURA, HOLD... ONNN...
!!!...

MAKE SURE THE REST ARE DEAD. I'M GOING AFTER--
THE VIRUS HAS BEEN DESTROYED.
SHE WAS GONNA JUMP IN A VAT OF MOLTEN METAL! I SAVED HER!
SHE DOESN'T LOOK SAVED, KID.
WHAT'S WITH ALL THE BURNS?
ELIXIR DROPPED ME. I CAUGHT FIRE WHEN I HIT THE EDGE OF THE TANK.
I SAID I WAS SORRY!
WHAT NOW?
NOW WE'RE GONNA BLOW THIS PLACE TO HELL.
AND THEN I'M GONNA FIND VANISHER AND CUT OFF HIS @#$%ING HEAD.

EPILOGUE ONE:
THE COLORADO ROCKY MOUNTAINS.
HURR... HURR... HUR--
RRRRAAA!!
WHOEVER YOU ARE...RUN. I DINNAE WANT TO KILL YE.

IF I MUST DIE, MY LOVE, THEN LET IT BE LOOKING UPON YOUR BEAUTY.
LONG HAVE I EEN SEARCHING OR YOU, RAHNE SINCLAIR.
H-HRIMHARI?...

EPILOGUE, TWO: WASHINGTON, D.C.
REPORT, MISTER HODGE.
WE FAILED TO ACQUIRE LOT 14 6, SPECIMEN NUMBER FIVE.
THE X-MEN GOT THERE BEFORE WE DID. THE SAMPLE WAS DESTROYED.
THAT IS... UNFORTUNATE.
I AGREE. BUT THE THREE REMAINING SPECIMENS TAKEN FROM SINISTER'S LABS IN ECUADOR, NEW YORK AND PERTH ARE IN OUR POSSESSION.
THE ECUADOR SAMPLE IS ALREADY SHOWING GREAT PROMISE.
REPLICATE THE SAMPLE AND SEE THAT IT REACHES THE LEPER QUEEN.

ANGEL'S AERIE.
VT!
--MRF!! MM RRRY!!
AND IF YOU EVER @*%$ING DO THAT AGAIN, I WILL--
WHAT THE HELL HAPPENED TO YOU?
MY NAME IS JAMES PROUDSTAR.
HE DUG UP JOHNNY...
HE TOOK MY ENTIRE TRIBE.
I DON'T WANT TO BE A KILLER.
WHO DID?
BUT NOW I HAVE NO CHOICE.
ELI BARD.

WHO THE HELL IS ELI BARD?

©

ANGEL'S AERIE. NOW.
WHO THE HELL IS ELI BARD?

HE'S THE MAN THAT WAS WITH RISMAN, THE MAN THAT ALMOST KILLED LAURA.
HE'S THE BASTARD THAT DUG UP THE GRAVES OF MY TRIBE AND DESECRATED THEIR BODIES.
THAT'S WHAT MADE THE DEMON BEAR MANIFEST. IT WAS BARD. THE SPIRITS SHOWED ME EVERYTHING. THEY SHOWED ME HIS WHOLE LIFE.

WOW, AND I THOUGHT WE WERE BUSY.
I HAVE NO IDEA WHAT THE HELL HE JUST SAID. WHAT'S A "GHOST BEAR?"
YOU GOT A STORY TO TELL, JIMMY, THEN TELL IT.
SOMETHING IS WRONG. WOLFSBANE IS NOT HERE.
WHAT? HANG ON, I'M COMING WITH YOU.

"IT STARTED ALMOST TWO THOUSAND YEARS AGO...
ROME.

"HIS NAME WAS
DIFFERENT THEN,
BUT IT WAS ELI..."

...OUR DUTY AS SENATORS... AS ROMANS...IS TO SUPPORT MASCIUS WHILE THE EMPEROR IS AWAY...

"HE WAS A HIGH-RANKING POLITICIAN.

"HE WAS RESPECTED BY THE MILITARY..."

...MARK MY WORDS, WARRIORS... WE NEED GOOD, HONORABLE MEN LIKE THIS IN THE SENATE, ENSURING THE DREAM WE FIGHT FOR ON THE BATTLEFIELD IS PROTECTED HERE AT HOME...

"...WEALTHY BEYOND MEASURE..."

PLEASE... PLEASE! FOR MY CHILDREN!

BACK, SCUM!!

SENATOR! WE ARE STARVING!!

"...A MEMBER OF THE ELITE...
CLAP!!-CLAP!!-CLAP!!-CLAP!!

MY HUSBAND...
"...AND LOVED BY ONE OF THE MOST POWERFUL WOMEN IN ALL OF ROME. HE HAD EVERYTHING..."

"...BUT IT WAS ALL A *LIE.*"
-GASP!-
IMBECILE!!
YOU STUPID, PATHETIC EXCU FOR A MAN! YO LITTLE "SPEEC TO THE SENAT ALMOST RUINE EVERYTHING!
AURELIA, PLEASE...
SILENCE! YOU HUMILIATED MASCIUS IN FRON OF EVERYONE!
HAD HE NOT BEEN THERE TO CONTROL THINGS, HE WOULD HAVE BEEN *RUINED.*
I MEANT NO--
GET OUT OF MY SIGHT.
WHAT? NO...I WILL NOT LEAVE MY OWN HOUSE.
YOUR HOUSE? DO NOT FORGET WHOSE HOUSE THIS REALLY IS. DO NOT FORGET WHO PAYS FOR YOUR LIFE. WHEN I FOUND YOU, YOU WERE A STARVING *POET.* IF NOT FOR *ME,* YOU WOULD BE BEGGING FOR FOOD AT THE MARKETPLACE.
BUT...
HAVE THE SLAVES POLISH THESE ON YOUR WAY OUT.
NOW BE GONE. MASCIUS AND I HAVE... BUSINESS...TO ATTEND TO.
INTERRUPT US, AND I'LL MAKE YOU FAN US WHILE WE WORK.

"BARD WAS A PATHETIC LITTLE MAN, PUT INTO POWER BY PEOPLE WHO WANTED NOTHING MORE THAN TO USE HIM."
ELIPHAS...

ELIPHAS...
IS...IS SOMEONE THERE?

YOU STARTLED ME, CHILD!
PLEASE, I AM SORRY...
IT'S ALRIGHT. WHAT IS YOUR NAME, GIRL?

CLAUDIA.
A STRONG NAME. HERE, YOU LOOK LIKE YOU COULD USE A MEAL.
MY PARENTS... THEY ARE HUNGRY, TOO. MAY I BRING IT BACK TO THEM?

YES, OF COURSE... TAKE THESE BACK TO THEM, TOO.
I...I...
YOU ARE MOST WELCOME.
NOW BE OFF BEFORE YOUR MASTERS DISCOVER YOU'VE GONE MISSING.

OOOO... MASCIUS... **MASCIUS!!**
"HE WASN'T AN EVIL MAN. HE WASN'T MAN ENOUGH TO EVEN MAKE THE CHOICE. IT WAS GOING TO BE MADE FOR HIM."

FOR THE LOVE OF GOD, PROUDSTAR, PLEASE TELL ME THIS IS GOING SOMEWHERE.
LET'S NOT BE TOO HASTY. I WANT TO HEAR MORE ABOUT THIS "MASCIUS" GUY. I LIKE HIS STYLE.
THIS IS WHERE IT'S GOING. TRUST ME...YOU'RE NOT GOING TO LIKE IT.

"SO THIS GUY HITS BOTTOM.

"HIS ENTIRE LIFE IS A SHAM. AND HE KNOWS THEY ALL KNOW IT. THEY'RE ALL LAUGHING AT HIM.

"AND THAT'S WHEN IT HAPPENS."
ELIPHAS...

WHAT...

I HAVE BEEN WAITING FOR YOU...

GREETINGS, ELIPHAS.
DO... DO I KNOW YOU?
NO, BUT I WANT YOU TO.
WILL YOU HONOR ME WITH YOUR COMPANY, ELIPHAS?
WHO ARE YOU?
I HAVE MANY NAMES. YOU MAY CALL ME SELENE.
RAAAA!! YOU HAVE GOT TO BE KIDDING ME!!
WHO THE HELL IS SELENE?
AN IMMORTAL MUTANT. BLACK QUEEN OF THE HELLFIRE CLUB. BAD NEWS.

"I WISH THIS WAS A JOKE, LOGAN. BELIEVE ME, YOU HAVE NO IDEA HOW BAD THIS STORY GETS."
MY LADY SELENE...I HAVE NEVER SEEN A CARRIAGE LIKE THIS BEFORE.
IF I MAY ASK, WHAT BUSINESS BRINGS YOU TO OUR FINE CITY?
IT IS NOT FROM ROME. AND NEITHER AM I, ELIPHAS.
I HAVE COME HERE FOR *YOU.*
I SEE...IS THERE SOME WAY THAT THE SENATE CAN HELP YOU, SOME--
NO. ONLY *YOU* CAN HELP ME. BUT I DO NOT SEEK THE MAN THAT SITS BEFORE ME.
I'M AFRAID I DON'T UNDERSTAND.
YOU WERE ONCE A GOOD MAN BEFORE THIS WICKED CITY CORRUPTED YOU. YOU WERE A GREAT SOLDIER BEFORE POLITICS SOFTENED YOU.
AND NOT SO LONG AGO, YOU HAD THE ABILITY TO LOVE...DEEPLY, PASSIONATELY AND BEAUTIFULLY, BEFORE YOUR HEART WAS BROKEN.
THIS MAN, THIS IS WHO I HAVE COME FOR.
HOW-- HOW DO YOU KNOW ALL THIS?
BECAUSE I WAS THERE. I WAS THERE THE DAY YOU WERE BORN. THE DAY YOU FIRST TOOK A MAN'S LIFE AS A SOLDIER, AND THE DAY WHEN A SPEAR BROKE YOUR BODY, ENDING YOUR YEARS ON THE BATTLEFIELD. I WAS THERE WHEN YOU FELL IN LOVE, AND THERE AGAIN WHEN SHE BROKE YOUR HEART.
I HAVE BEEN WAITING FOR YOU SINCE BEFORE THERE WAS A ROME.
I HAVE ALWAYS BEEN THERE, ELIPHAS. AND NOW IT IS TIME FOR US TO BEGIN OUR JOURNEY *TOGETHER.*
NO...WHAT YOU SAY IS IMPOSSIBLE.

I HAVE LIVED FOR THOUSANDS OF YEARS, ELIPHAS... AND I OFFER YOU THE SAME.
I CAN MAKE YOU YOUNG, HEALTHY AND STRONGER THAN YOU CAN IMAGINE. I CAN MAKE YOU IMPERVIOUS TO THE ILLS AND SUFFERING OF MORTALS, AND THAT IS JUST THE BEGINNING.
IN TIME, YOU WILL HAVE THE POWER TO CONTROL THE BEASTS OF THE NIGHT...
...AND THE ELEMENTS THEMSELVES.
YOU WILL LIVE A LIFE ETERNAL, AND HAVE MY LOVE FOR ALL TIME. AN AGELESS LOVE THAT WILL BE AS BEAUTIFUL AND PASSIONATE TODAY AS IT WILL BE 10,000 YEARS FROM NOW.
AND WHAT WOULD YOU ASK OF ME IN RETURN?
EVERY SOUL IN ROME.

"HE KNEW WHAT WAS HAPPENING. HE WAS A WORM, BUT HE KNEW TRUE EVIL WHEN HE SAW IT. AND IT SCARED HIM.

"MAYBE HE WOULD HAVE DONE THE RIGHT THING... MAYBE HE WOULD HAVE EVEN MADE THE RIGHT CHOICE."

MASCIUS? WHAT ARE--

"BUT FATE MADE THE CHOICE FOR HIM."

WE WERE SURPRISED TO HEAR YOU WERE STEPPING DOWN, ELIPHAS. THE PEOPLE OF ROME SHALL MISS YOUR SERVICE.

BUT WE ARE GLAD THAT YOU CHOSE MASCIUS TO TAKE YOUR SEAT.

MY SEAT... MASCIUS, WHAT--?

YOU ARE ***STEPPING DOWN*** AND NEED ME TO TAKE OVER YOUR DUTIES HERE IMMEDIATELY, THOSE WERE YOUR WORDS TO ME.

I--OF COURSE, MASCIUS. FORGIVE... ME.

FORGIVEN. OH, AND AURELIA ASKED FOR YOU. SHE HAS EXCITING NEWS.

YOU MAY DIE NOW, ELIPHAS.
BURN ALONG WITH YOUR POSSESSIONS, FOR ALL I CARE. I HAVE NEED OF YOU NO LONGER.

"THEY SAY A MAN WITH NOTHING LEFT TO LOSE IS THE MOST DANGEROUS MAN OF ALL."

...WHATEVER YOU REQUIRE, MY QUEEN.
ELIPHAS...I REQUIRE ONLY GODHOOD.
TOMORROW THE ARENA WILL HOST THE LARGEST BATTLE THE CITY HAS EVER SEEN. THOUSANDS OF SOULS AT ONCE...AND THEY ARE ONLY THE BEGINNING.

I'VE SHOWN YOU THE SIGILS, THE RUNES...TAKE MY BLADE. YOU KNOW WHAT TO DO.
TOGETHER, WE WILL LIVE FOREVER.

FIVE POINTS OF A PENTAGRAM... ALL OF ROME WILL BURN. THEY WILL PAY FOR WHAT...
THEY WILL ALL PAY...

"IN THIS TIME, ELI WASN'T EVIL. JUST WEAK."
GODS SAVE ME.

"BUT ONE MOMENT OF KINDNESS CHANGED EVERYTHING."
TELL NO ONE BUT YOUR FAMILY, AND YOU MUST GO NOW...

SENATOR...
SENATOR!

TAKE YOUR FILTHY HAND OFF ME, SLAVE...
MY LORD, PLEASE...YOU MUST LISTEN.
SOMETHING TERRIBLE IS GOING TO HAPPEN, PLEASE... YOUR FRIEND ELIPHAS...
FATHER, PLEASE, I CANT!
TELL HIM NOW!

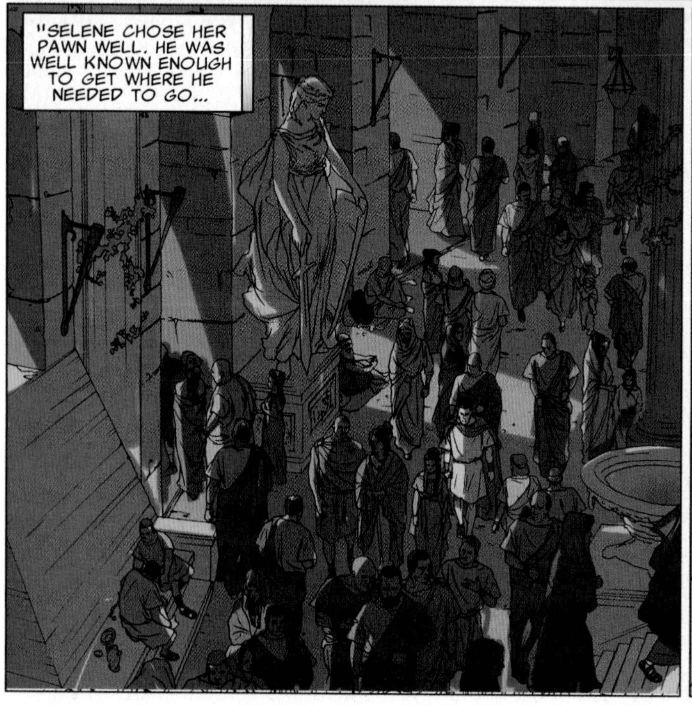
"SELENE CHOSE HER PAWN WELL. HE WAS WELL KNOWN ENOUGH TO GET WHERE HE NEEDED TO GO...

"...BUT AT THE SAME TIME NO ONE CARED ENOUGH TO ASK WHY HE WAS GOING THERE."

HNH!
EVERY SOUL...
EVERY SOUL IN ROME...AND SHE WILL BE REBORN A GODDESS.
AND SHE WILL LOVE ME FOREVER.
"SELENE'S PLAN WAS SIMPLE. SE ELI TO HELP CAST A SPELL THAT WOULD ALLOW HER TO DEVOUR TENS OF THOUSANDS OF SOULS, ALL AT ONCE.
"ONE LIFE GIVES SELENE POWER, WE'VE SEEN IT HAPPEN.
"TAKING THAT MANY LIVES WOULD MAKE HER A *GOD*."

TOGETHER... UHH...WE WILL LIVE... FOREVER--
WHAM!!
UHNN!!
LIVE FOREVER? MY DEAR FRIEND...
"...YOU WON'T SURVIVE THE NIGHT."
CALLIDUS!
CALLIDUS!
CALLIDUS!
"THIS WAS ELI'S LAST DAY AS A HUMAN.

"NO ONE KNOWS WHERE SELENE CAME FROM.
"WHO SHE IS, WHAT SHE IS...

"SHE CLAIMS SHE'S OLDER THAN MANKIND. MAYBE SHE'S A MUTANT, AN EXTERNAL, ONE OF THE FIRST. LIKE APOCALYPSE, MAYBE...I DON'T KNOW.
"BUT WHATEVER SHE IS, SHE WANTS TO BE MORE.

SHE WANTS POWER, SHE WANTS TO BE WORSHIPPED AS A GODDESS.

"MAYBE SHE COULD HAVE DONE IT...BUT SHE MADE ONE MISTAKE."
NO...NO! THIS CANNOT BE--

AAAAIIIEEEE!!

NO!!!
ONE WOULD THINK A WITCH COULD DO BETTER THAN YOU, ELIPHAS.
DO YOU BELIEVE YOU CAN KILL ME, HUMANS?
I CAN NEVER DIE! AND I WILL HAVE YOUR--
HURKK!
BIND THE BODY, TAKE THEM OUTSIDE THE CITY...
AND THEN BURN THEM AT THE STAKE.
NO...NO! SELENE... SELENE!!

"IF ONLY IT WERE SO EASY."

...PLEASE, I BEG THEE... HAVE MERCY... PLEASE, HAVE MERCY ON ME...

ENJOY HELL, VERMIN.
NO!!

NOOOO!!

HSSS...

WHOOOOSH!!
AAAIEEE!!
AAAAHHH!

AAAAHHHH... AHHHH...HELP ME... OH, GODS, HELP MEEE!
ELIPHASSSS... NO GOD CAN HELP YOU NOW.

AAAHHH!
LOOK AT WHAT YOU'VE DONE TO ME! LOOK AT ME!!
I'M SORRY... I'M SORRY...I DIDN'T MEAN...

I OFFER YOU EVERYTHING, AND YOU BETRAY ME!
PLEASE, I DID NOT WANT THIS...I ONLY WANTED A LIFE ETERNAL WITH YOU BY MY--
OH, YOU WILL HAVE LIFE ETERNAL, ELIPHAS... A LIFE OF ETERNAL TORMENT.

YYEARRRGGH!!
YOU WILL LIVE FOREVER, AND FOREVER I WILL DENY DEATH TO YOU. I WILL DENY MY PRESENCE TO YOU.
PRAY YOU NEVER SEE ME AGAIN.

NNOOOO!

SEVEN HUNDRED YEARS LATER.
CHOK!
WHAT IN THE NAME OF ALL THAT'S HOLY...
AAAAHHHH!
SELENE.

"FOR HUNDREDS OF YEARS, HE WALKED THE EARTH, LOOKING FOR SELENE. AFTER EVERYTHING SHE DID TO HIM, HE STILL LOVED HER.
"AND EVERYWHERE HE WENT, HE BROUGHT DEATH.
"EVENTUALLY HE LEFT THE OLD WORLD, FOLLOWING SELENE'S TRAIL TO THE NEW.
"THERE HE FOUND MY PEOPLE, WHO RECOGNIZED HIM FOR WHAT HE WAS.
"THEY WERE UNABLE TO DEFEAT HIM AND THEIR DEATHS WERE BLAMED ON THE DISEASES BROUGHT TO OUR LANDS BY THE COLONISTS.
"HE WAS GETTING CLOSER AND CLOSER TO HER, TRACKING HER ALL THE WAY TO THE PRESENT DAY...HE FOUND HER IN NOVA ROMA.
"BUT HE WAS TOO AFRAID TO APPROACH HER. TOO SACRED OF HER WRATH. HE NEEDED SOMETHING TO APPEASE HER. AN OFFERING.
"AND FINALLY, HE FOUND ONE. A SACRIFICE THAT EVEN SELENE COULDN'T IGNORE.
"THE PURIFIERS. THOUSANDS OF THEM."

HE WAS GOING TO USE THIS BLADE AGAIN AND CAST THE SAME SPELL. HE PLANNED TO SACRIFICE THE PURIFIERS' BLACK SOULS TO SELENE. EVERY LAST ONE OF THEM. HE WANTED TO MAKE HER A GODDESS. HE WANTED HER TO LOVE HIM AGAIN.
THAT'S ALL HE CARES ABOUT NOW.
ROMANTIC. MESSED UP, BUT ROMANTIC.
YOU KNOW WHAT? SCREW YOU GUYS. I'LL TAKE MY CHANCES WITH THE TUMOR.
WHAT DOES THIS HAVE TO DO WITH THE TECHNARCH. OR YOUR TRIBE?
EVERYTHING.

NEW ORLEANS.
NOW.
MY QUEEN...I HAVE MISSED YOU.
YOU'VE MADE A TERRIBLE MISTAKE COMING BACK TO ME, ELIPHAS.
KILL HIM, MY CHILDREN.
MY QUEEN... I HAVE AN OFFERING FOR YOU.
I DO NOT KNOW WHAT FOUL SCIENCE HAS GIVEN YOU THESE SLAVES, BUT I HAVE NO NEED OF THEM.
MY QUEEN...YOU MISUNDERSTAND. THEY ARE NOT MY OFFERING...

THIS IS A DEAD MUTANT CALLED CALIBAN. IN LIFE HE COULD TRACK ANY MUTANT ON THE PLANET, BUT IN DEATH, HE CAN FIND ALL THOSE LOST TO THE WORLD.
ONCE FOUND, I WILL RESURRECT THOSE MUTANTS JUST AS I DID THIS APACHE AND HIS TRIBE.
IT IS THOSE MUTANTS...THEIR POWER...AND THEIR SOULS...THAT I OFFER YOU.

AMES, IOWA.

THIS IS WHAT IS AT STAKE!
IT REMINDS ME OF ANOTHER TIME.
OUR FUTURE. OUR VERY WAY OF LIFE.
THIS IS WHAT THE MUTANT THREAT IS.
WHEN MUTANTS WERE SOMETHING YOU ONLY HEARD ABOUT ON TV.

AND GRAYDON CREED IS ONE OF THE FEW BRAVE ENOUGH TO DO ANYTHING ABOUT IT. HE'S ONE OF THE FEW WHO WILL STAND UP TO THEM.
HE'S BEEN TARGETED BY MUTANTS BEFORE, BUT HE WON'T STOP FIGHTING FOR YOU.
BEFORE ONE OF THEM DESTROYED MY LIFE, BURNING DOWN EVERYTHING I EVER CARED ABOUT.

AND WHEN HE ARRIVES, GRAYDON CREED WILL TELL YOU ABOUT THE FRIENDS OF HUMANITY.
A MUTANT WILL KILL HER...BUT IT WON'T BE A MUTANT'S FAULT.
HE'LL TELL YOU ABOUT THE LIST OF MUTANTS THE GOVERNMENT HAS, HOW THEY KNOW WHERE THEY ARE...HOW... WHAT IN--?
SECURITY... WE NEED SECURITY HERE...
I WAS BEAUTIFUL LIKE THIS GIRL, ONCE. AND NOW SHE'S GOING TO DIE, LIKE THE PERSON I WAS DIED.
HEY...GET AWAY...GET AWAY FROM ME!
WHAT IS-- I--WHERE AM I?

AAAAH!!!
AAAIIIIEEE!!
NO! NO! NOOOO!!
WHO ARE YOU?! WHO ARE YOU?!
ALL OF THESE PEOPLE... THEY'RE GOING TO DIE. THEY'RE GOING TO DIE AT A MUTANT'S HANDS, AND IT'S MY FAULT.
PLEASE, HELP ME... HELP ME...IT'S INSIDE ME, PLEASE...
WE FOUND THE FILTH TRAVELLING WEST THROUGH ST. LOUIS, HEADING TO SAN FRANCISCO. THAT'S WHERE THEIR KIND LIVE NOW.
I SHOULD HAVE KILLED IT RIGHT THEN AND THERE.
PLEASE...I DON'T WANT TO DIE.
I SHOULD HAVE KILLED MYSELF WITH HER.

UT!
ELEVEN HUNDRED HUMANS DEAD. ALL OF THEM MURDERED BY ME.
MY NAME IS THE LEPER QUEEN. I KILL MUTANTS.
AND THIS... THIS IS *WRONG.*

ST. LOUIS. DIVISION C OF THE ORGANIZATION FORMERLY KNOWN AS 'S.H.I.E.L.D.'
THE PURIFIERS RESCUED THE LEPER QUEEN AS SHE WAS BOUT TO BE EXECUTED FOR MURDERING A MUTANT.

PIERCE WAS ABDUCTED BY THEM AS WELL. AND NOW THAT WILLIAM STRYKER HAS RESURFACED, MATTHEW RISMAN HAS FALLEN OFF THE GRID.
FOR THE SAKE OF ARGUMENT, LET'S SAY X-23 IS INVOLVED IN THE PURIFIER MASSACRES.

LET'S SAY IT'S ALL CONNECTED.

OUR INTEL BACKS UP ALL OF THOSE ASSUMPTIONS... SO HOW DO YOU SUGGEST WE TRACK HER?

SHE'S A MUTANT, AN ASSASSIN FOR HIRE, AND IS NOW GOING AFTER A MUTANT HATE GROUP.

WE WORK AHEAD OF HER. FIND HER NEXT TARGET.

AGENT MORALES, SORRY TO INTERRUPT... BUT WE'VE GOT A RED FLAG. YOU... YOU SHOULD REALLY SEE THIS.

THERE'S BEEN AN INCIDENT AT A RALLY...

GRAYMALKIN INDUSTRIES, MARIN.
STATUS?
SHE'S SITTING DOWN FOR LUNCH IN BARCELONA.
SHE'S THINKING ABOUT DESSERT.
SHE'S THINKING ABOUT YOU.
ANY LUCK WITH WOLFSBANE?
WE'VE BEEN TRYING TO TRACK HER FOR DAYS. IT IS VERY ODD.
WE CAN FEEL HER, BUT SHE DOES NOT REGISTER ON CEREBRA.
HER SIGNAL IS SKETCHY.
WE WONDER IF SHE IS IN WOLF FORM.
KEEP ON IT, GIRLS. REPORT BACK.
WHAT HAVE YOU GOT, HANK?

TIME TRAVEL THE PALM OF YOUR HAND.
OR *PAW*, AS THE CASE MAY BE.
I'M IMPRESSED. I THOUGHT YOU WERE HAVING TROUBLE REPLICATING FORGE'S WORK.
I HAVEN'T GIVEN YOU THE FINE PRINT YET.
OUR LITTLE "SCIENCE" TEAM ARE SOME OF THE GREATEST MINDS ON EARTH, BUT FORGE IS FORGE. THIS ISN'T ON THE SAME LEVEL AS WHAT HE CREATED.

I CAN'T HELP BUT NOTICE YOU'RE NOT TELLING ME *WHO* THE DEVICES ARE FOR.
NO, I'M NOT.
SCOTT, I KNOW WHAT'S AT STAKE, I KNOW HOW IMPORTANT CABLE'S MISSION IS. I KNOW WHAT THE BABY MEANS FOR US ALL.
HANK...
BUT IF YOU'RE PLANNING ON EXECUTING BISHOP, I WANT NO PART OF THIS.
YOU HAVE TO TRUST ME ON THIS.
ALRIGHT, I'LL HAVE THE DEVICES FOR YOU IN A FEW HOURS.
HEY, GUYS.
SCOTT, CAN I BORROW YOU FOR A MINUTE?

ALCATRAZ.
WILL YOU CALM DOWN, JIMMY?
IF YOU DON'T BREATHE SOON, I'M GONNA HAVE TO KILL YOU.
WE SHOULD BE OUT THERE--
JUST WAIT. HE'S HERE.
DID YOU FIND THEM?
RAHNE? BARD? SELENE? HAVE YOU FOUND ANY OF THEM? HAVE YOU DONE ANYTHING?
THE CUCKOOS ARE WORKING ON IT, WARPATH. I PROMISE. BUT THIS TAKES PRIORITY.
PRIORITY?! WHAT THE HELL IS MORE IMPORTANT THAN--
WHERE ARE THE OTHERS?
VT!
HAHA HAHA HA!!!
IT'S NOT FUNNY, DAMMIT!!
SHE CUT OFF MY $*#@ING EAR!!

ANY PARTICULAR REASON?
HE ATTEMPTED TO BRIBE ELIXIR INTO REMOVING THE TUMOR. HE HAD TO BE PUNISHED.
SHE'S PSYCHOTIC!!
SHUT UP, ALL OF YOU. WE HAVE A PROBLEM.
BEAUTIFUL DREAMER IS DEAD.
WHO THE *@(# IS BEAUTIFUL DREAMER?
SHE WAS A MORLOCK. NOT EVEN WORTH KILLING.
WHAT HAPPENED?
IT HAPPENED AT A FRIENDS OF HUMANITY RALLY FOR GRAYDON CREED. SHE KILLED HUNDREDS OF PEOPLE, THEN DIED.
BULL. WHAT DOES SHE DO, WIPE MEMORIES? SHE'S NO KILLER.
EVERYONE IN RANGE, THEIR MINDS WERE WIPED. THEIR BRAINS FORGOT TO TELL THEIR HEARTS TO BEAT.
HER POWERS, THEY WERE OUT OF CONTROL. THEY FLARED, AN IT KILLED HER.
THERE'S SOMETHING THAT DOES THAT TO MUTANTS...
...THE LEGACY VIRUS.

NO. NOT POSSIBLE.
THE VIRUS DOESN'T WORK THAT FAST, AND WE ESTROYED ALL THE MPLES IN SINISTER'S LAB. HELL, WE DESTROYED THE LAB.

NOT TO BE A DOWNER OR ANYTHING, BUT WE KNOW SINISTER HAD MORE LABS. COULD HE HAVE HAD MORE SAMPLES OF THE VIRUS?

I DON'T KNOW. BUT THE FRIENDS OF HUMANITY ARE PUTTING IT OUT THERE THAT THEY'VE RECEIVED THREATS FROM MUTANT TERRORISTS.
ALL OF THEIR RALLIES HAVE BEEN TARGETED. AND I WANT YOU THERE.

IF THIS IS BASTION AND THE LEGACY VIRUS, WE HAVE TO STOP IT. PERMANENTLY.

REALLY? ARE YOU SURE YOU DON'T WANT TO STOP IT TEMPORARILY?
GOD, YOU IDIOTS LOVE YOUR DRAMA.

GRAYMALKIN INDUSTRIES. CELL BLOCK 'X'.
IS THE DOG BOY STILL DEAD? I KNOW YOU MUTANTS HAVE A NASTY HABIT OF COMING BACK TO LIFE.
DO YOU HAVE NO SOUL AT ALL?
THAT'S WHAT YOU'RE GOING TO ASK ME? YOU'RE OUT OF YOUR LEAGUE, GIRL. THE OTHERS HAD MUCH BETTER QUESTIONS FOR ME.
WHAT OTHERS? WHAT ARE YOU TALKING ABOUT?
YOU REALLY DON'T KNOW, DO YOU? IT LOOKS LIK YOUR FEARLESS LEADER IS KEEPING SECRETS.
THAT'S FUNNY.
YOU ARE MAD.
MAYBE I AM. AFTER ALL...
...I WAS DEFEATED BY CHILDREN AND NOW I ROT HERE IN YOUR LITTLE JAILHOUSE.
IT'S ENOUGH TO DRIVE ANYONE MAD.
UPLOADING.

WASHINGTON, D.C.
RECEIVING DATA.
RECORDING SCHEMATICS, INHABITANTS... GREYMALKIN INDUSTRIES.
CROSS-LINK, SAPIEN LEAGUE.
I DON'T UNDERSTAND.
I DON'T UNDERSTAND WHY SO MANY HUMANS HAVE TO DIE! AND FOR WHAT?!
IT IS A REQUIRED DISTRACTION, GRAYDON CREED. THIS WILL KEEP THE X-MEN OCCUPIED UNTIL IT IS TOO LATE.
UNTIL JUDGMENT DAY.
SO ALL OF THIS, MY ENTIRE EXISTENCE... THE OTHERS... WE'RE JUST A "DISTRACTION"?
NOT ALL OF YOU.

I SHOULD BE GLAD I'M ALIVE. BUT NOT LIKE THIS. NOT AS SOMETHING LESS THAN HUMAN.
BEING FORCED TO DO *THIS.*
I CAN FEEL IT, UNDER MY SKIN. I CAN FEEL *HIM,* LISTENING INSIDE MY HEAD.
AM I INSANE? IS MY MIND AS SCARRED AS MY FACE? I DON'T KNOW WHO I AM ANYMORE. SOME KIND OF MONSTER...
NO. I KNOW WHO I AM, AND *THEY* ARE THE MONSTERS. I WAS PUT ON THIS EART TO ***KILL MUTANT.*** AND I WILL NOT DO THIS.
HE CAN'T MAKE ME KILL THESE PEOPLE!

LET'S GO.

LOCATION UNKNOWN.

MY SAPIEN LEAGUE WAS EASY ENOUGH TO RE-FORM. SMALL-MINDED PEOPLE, BLAMING ALL THEIR PROBLEMS ON MUTANTS. LOSE THEIR JOB, LOSE THEIR GIRLFRIEND...A MUTANT IS TO BLAME.

IT'S SAD. BUT IT MAKES THEM EASY TO USE. THEY HAVE NO IDEA WHAT THE MUTANTS ARE CAPABLE OF. THEY HAVEN'T SEEN THE FACE OF APOCALYPSE LIKE I HAVE.

WHAT IS THIS STUFF?

MAKES MUTANTS SICK. MAKES THEM DIE. THAT'S ALL YOU NEED TO KNOW.

HUH. CAN WE GET MORE OF IT?

CAMERON HODGE IS PROBABLY MAKING IT BY THE BARREL. HE'S ONE OF US. ONE OF *HIS*.

WE'RE GIVEN A FACE AND A LOCATION. WE ABDUCT THE MUTANT. INJECT THEM.

AND TURN THEM LOOSE AT A SPECIFIED PLACE AND TIME.

UHN!!
PART OF HIS "MASTER PLAN."
CHK!!
PLEASE...IF THERE IS A GOD...
...LET ME DIE.

HRIMHARI, MY PRINCE... IS THIS A DREAM?
I HAD HEARD ABOUT ASGARD APPEARING ON EARTH, BUT I NEVER THOUGHT... H-HOW CAN YOU BE HERE...WITH ME?
WHEN ASGARD FELL, I FELL WITH IT.
"I WAS LOCKED IN COMBAT WITH A FROST GIANT WAR PARTY. THE SAVAGES HUNTED DOWN AND MURDERED MY ENTIRE PACK.
"THE PELTS OF MY LOVED ONES, STILL WET WITH INNOCENT BLOOD, HUNG FROM THEIR BELTS WHEN I FOUND THEM. I HAD LITTLE HOPE OF KILLING THE BEASTS BUT I COULD NOT LET THEM ESCAPE."
BUT THEN I FELT SOMETHING... A SENSATION MORE POWERFUL THAN ANYTHING I HAVE EVER KNOWN...
AND WHEN I TURNED TO SEE WHAT IT WAS...
"...I FOUND RAGNAROK.
"THE END OF ALL THINGS HAD COME AS FORETOLD...AND IN AN INSTANT, EVERY IMMORTAL LIFE WAS EXTINGUISHED, MINE INCLUDED. BUT THEN...
"...LIFE RETURNED.
"I FOUND MYSELF IN MY OWN LANDS, BUT LOOKING OUT ACROSS MIDGARD.
"I CANNOT EXPLAIN HOW I RETURNED TO THE LIVING BUT I DO KNOW WHY I WAS REBORN ON MIDGARD."

WHY?
FOR YOU.
RAHNE, DO YOU REMEMBER THE FIRST TIME I LOST YOU? WHEN LOKI, THE GOD OF EVIL, MADE YOU CHOOSE BETWEEN OUR LOVE AND YOUR FRIENDS?
AYE. IT IS CHOICE I HAVE HOUGHT ABOUT VERY DAY SINCE I WAS FORCED TO MAKE IT.
"DO YOU REMEMBER WHAT I SAID WHEN I KNEW THAT I WOULD LOSE YOU?"
"YOU--YOU SAID THAT I WAS YOUR 'HEART'... THAT I WAS YOUR 'LIFE.'"
"TRUER WORDS, I HAVE NEVER SPOKEN."
IN THE MOMENTS BEFORE MY LIFE ENDED, MY ONLY THOUGHT WAS OF YOU. YOU ARE MY LIFE, RAHNE. OUR FATES ARE INTERTWINED AND NOT EVEN DEATH COULD KEEP US APART.
I AM AND ALWAYS HAVE BEEN YOURS...
THAT IS, IF YOU WILL HAVE M-- RFF!!

JACKSON HOLE, WYOMING.

"THIS IS NOT A FEASIBLE SURVEILLANCE SOLUTION."

THERE ARE TOO MANY PEOPLE. OUR SENSES ARE USELESS IN A CROWD LIKE THIS.

I DIDN'T KNOW ASSASSINS COMPLAINED THIS MUCH.

YOU SHOULD BE IN THE AIR. YOUR FILE LISTS YOUR VISUAL RANGE AT--

I CAN SMELL THE DEATH. I'M STAYING RIGHT HERE.

BOISE, IDAHO.
SHUT UP, BOTH OF YOU!
JUST GET THE JOB DONE!

PROVIDENCE, RHODE ISLAND.
OKAY, JAMES... HERE'S A THOUGHT. THERE'S A ONE-IN-THREE CHANCE A MUTANT BOMB IS GOING TO GO OFF HERE.
SO HOW ABOUT YOU AND I NOT BE HERE? WE COULD GO SOMEPLACE SUNNY. I KNOW THIS BROTHEL IN PORTUGAL...
JUST BE READY, TELFORD.

IT'LL BE DOM AND LOGAN THAT FINDS THEM, ANYWAY.

SHE'S GOT LUCK ON HER SIDE.

WELL, IF SHE'S LUCKY, IT **WON'T** BE HER. BECAUSE WHOEVER FINDS THEM IS GOING TO **DIE**.

WILL YOU ALL SHUT UP!?!

I DO NOT...

THIS IS NOT RIGHT.

WHAT'S THE MATTER? ARE YOU GETTING SOMETHING?

SNFF
TALK TO ME!
SOMETHING IS BURNING.
HEY!
WHUMP!
WARREN! LAURA! WHAT'S HAPPENING?!

AAIIEEE!!
MUTANT!!

AAAHHH!!

OH, GOD... IT BURNS! THIS ISN'T HAPPENING! I'M BURNING!!
SOMEBODY HELP ME!!!

FEVER PITCH. ACOLYTE. IF HIS POWERS FLARE...
KILL HIM!
THERE'S NOT ENOUGH TIME.
PORTER! PULL THEM OUT NOW!!
AAAAHHH!

SUGAR CAFE, SAN FRANCISCO.
JULIAN KELLER, A.K.A. HELLION.
AM I A MUTANT? SWEETHEART...
...I'M ONE OF THE MOST POWERFUL MUTANTS ON THE PLANET.
REALLY? I KNEW IT... I CAN JUST TELL.
SO WHAT ARE YOU DOING TONIGHT?
I'M LOOKING...AT... HERRRRR...
NO. WHAT YOU'RE DOING TONIGHT IS DYING, YOU GENESCUM PIECE OF $#!^.
SCREECH!
CONTACT THE LEPER QUEEN.
TELL HER WE'VE GOT EVERYONE ON THE LIST.

JACKSON HOLE, WYOMING.
ONE HOUR AGO.
MY NAME IS WOLVERINE. THIS EVIL BASTARD IS FEVER PITCH...
...AND FOR THE SECOND TIME IN TWO DAYS, A MUTANT HAS JUST KILLED A WHOLE LOT OF HUMANS.
ODDS ARE, ANY NORMAL DAY, HE'D ENJOY KILLING HUMANS.

BUT WHAT HAPPENED HERE WASN'T HIS IDEA.

SAN FRANCISCO BAY. ALCATRAZ ISLAND.
HUNDREDS OF PEOPLE WERE KILLED, SCOTT.
THE THEORY IS, BOTH HIM AND BEAUTIFUL DREAMER WERE FILLED TO THE GILLS WITH A MODIFIED VERSION OF THE LEGACY VIRUS CREATED BY SINISTER.
THE SAME ONE WE SUPPOSEDLY DESTROYED.
IT WAS...IT WAS...
GOD. LOOK AT WORTHINGTON. HE WANTS TO SAY HE LOVED IT. THAT HE LOVED SEEING ALL THOSE PEOPLE DEAD.
HE'S TWISTED UP INSIDE. CYKE THINKS HE CAN SHAKE IT, I DID TOO...BUT NOW I'M NOT SO SURE.
IT WAS HORRIBLE. WE BARELY MADE IT OUT. BUT I SAW HER.
SAW WHO?
"THE LEPER QUEEN."
THAT CHANGES THINGS.
SUMMERS. HE'S SO HARDCORE LATELY, I'M STARTING TO FEEL INADEQUATE. I CAN SEE THE WHEELS TURNING IN HIS HEAD...WE BOTH KNOW WHERE THIS IS GOING.
QUESTION IS, HOW BLOODY DO HIS HANDS GET STOPPING IT?
SHE WAS GONE WHEN WE LANDED...AND BY THAT TIME, VANISHER HAD GOTTEN THE REST OF THE TEAM TO THE SITE. ELIXIR HELPED EVERYONE HE COULD BEFORE WE HAD TO GET OUT...
WE'RE X-FORCE. OUR HANDS ARE SUPPOSED TO GET BLOODY.
BUT HE'S THE ONE CALLING THE SHOTS.

SHE'S ONE OF BASTION'S.
'COURSE, CYKE ISN'T SAYING THE COLD TRUTH, THERE'S NO POINT. WE ALL KNOW IT.
BASTION HAS THE LEGACY VIRUS, AND WE'RE ALL *%#$ED.
SO...SEEMS LIKE WE'RE ALL *%#$ED.
THANKS, DOM.
THIS DOESN'T MAKE SENSE. SO THE LEPER QUEEN IS OUT THERE ABDUCTING MUTANTS, TURNING THE INTO LIVING BOMBS... FOR WHAT? TO USE AGAINST HUMANS?
THAT'S THE OPPOSITE OF WHO SHE IS. SO WHY?
HATE AND FEAR. IT'LL CREATE AN ANTI-MUTANT HYSTERIA. BETWEEN THIS AND THE LEAK OF THE COOPERSTOWN FOOTAGE, IT'S THE OLD DAYS ALL OVER AGAIN.
I MAKE THE CALL, SO HE DOESN'T HAVE TO. SO HE DOESN'T HAVE TO SAY THE WORDS.
WE TRACK HER AND KILL HER.
THAT'S RIGHT. BUT SOMETHING ELSE HAS COME UP.
CABLE.
UH-OH.

WE'RE CLOSE TO FINDING HIM AND THE BABY. WHEN WE DO, I'M SENDING YOU IN TO HELP HIM.
HE STILL CAN'T BRING HIMSELF TO SAY THE WORDS.
KILL BISHOP.
IN THIS BAG ARE TIME DEVICES FOR EACH OF YOU. YOU'LL HAVE 33.2 HOURS TO COMPLETE YOUR MISSION--AFTER THAT YOU'LL BE BROUGHT BACK AUTOMATICALLY.
WHY?
FIRST MUTANT BABY SINCE M-DAY, AND BISHOP SNAPS. TRIES TO KILL IT. NOW HE'S CHASING CABLE ALL OVER THE FUTURE, TRYING TO TAKE THEM OUT.
HE CAME BACK FOR SUPPLIES. WE CAUGHT HIM, BUT IT WAS A TRICK. HE GOT WHATEVER IT WAS HE NEEDED, AND TOOK THE X-MEN DOWN A NOTCH DOING IT.
CYKE'S TAKING IT A LITTLE PERSONAL.
THE DEVICES ARE PROTOTYPES... WE DIDN'T HAVE MUCH TIME TO PUT THEM TOGETHER. THERE ARE SIDE EFFECTS.
WHAT, LIKE HEADACHES?
DEATH.
THAT'S... A HELL OF A SIDE EFFECT.
ARE YOU SERIOUS?! YOU KNOW WHAT? YOU CAN COUNT ME RIGHT THE @#$% OUT. NO TIME TRAVEL FOR THIS GUY. NO FREAKING WAY.
IF WE DON'T COME BACK, YOU DIE.
...
I #$%@ING HATE YOU.
EVERYONE GOES. WEAR THE DEVICES. BE READY.
WHEN WE FIND HIM, THERE WON'T BE MUCH TIME.
GREAT.

GRAYMALKIN INDUSTRIES, MARIN.
IT'S INEVITABLE NOW, YOU KNOW THAT, RIGHT?
WHAT IS?
KILLING YOU IS LIKE KILLING THE DODO.
YOU ONLY GET TO DO IT ONCE, SO YOU HAVE TO RELISH IT.
YOUR TAUNTS ARE NOT VERY EFFECTIVE FROM WITHIN A CELL, MONSTER.
FOR THAT VERY REASON, YOUR THREATS ARE MEANINGLESS TO ME.
YOU TELL ME YOU'RE DYING, BUT I ALREADY KNEW. YOU'RE ALL DYING. YOU JUST HAPPEN TO KNOW IT, GIRL.
OH, YOU DON'T NEED TO BE WORRIED. NOT ABOUT YOU.
I'D BE MUCH MORE CONCERNED ABOUT YOUR LITTLE FRIENDS...
...BECAUSE THREE OF THEM ARE GOING TO DIE LONG BEFORE YOU DO.

IT'S PROBABLY NOTHING, SOORAYA. LIKE YOU SAID, HE'S GONE MAD.
HIS ENHANCEMENTS MAKE HIS MIND IMPOSSIBLE TO READ.
HE USES VERY INAPPROPRIATE LANGUAGE, THOUGH.

BUT COULD HIS THREAT HAVE ANY BASIS IN REALITY? CAN YOU TRACK ALL OF THE STUDENTS?
ONE-SIXTH OF US ARE IN THIS ROOM, SOORAYA.

IT ISN'T DIFFICULT.
HMM... THREE MUTANT SIGNATURES ARE OUTSIDE THE CITY, HEADING TOWARD NEW YORK. THEY ARE UNCONSCIOUS.

WHO?
DON'T TELL HER. NO NAMES.
I...CANNOT TELL. THERE IS INTERFERENCE.
CONTACT WOLVERINE. GATHER X-FORCE.
TELL THEM THE LEPER QUEEN IS IN NEW YORK.

H.A.M.M.E.R., DIVISION 'C'.
H.A.M.M.E.R.
SHE'S GOING TO NEW YORK.
SHE'S GOT TWO POTENTIAL TARGETS THERE: THE LEPER QUEEN AND THE UNITED NATIONS.
STEPHEN LANG AND BOLIVAR TRASK WERE BOTH IN THE PROTECTION PROGRAM WITH CREED. THEY'RE MAKING A PRESENTATION TO THE U.N. FOR AN INTERNATIONAL MUTANT RESPONSE DIVISION.
AND THE LEPER QUEEN HAS APPARENTLY RESURFACED. A KNOWN SAPIEN LEAGUE ORGANIZER HAS BEEN SETTING UP IN THE CITY.
THIS IS IT. THE DEATH TOLL IS STILL COMING IN FROM JACKSON HOLE. IF X-23 IS INVOLVED--
SHE IS.
THEN WE CAN'T AFFORD TO LET HER ESCAPE THIS TIME. SHE'S GOTTEN AWAY WITH MURDER FOR FAR TOO LONG.
I'LL GET YOU TWO H.A.M.M.E.R. ASSAULT SQUADS IN NEW YORK IMMEDIATELY.

ANGEL'S AERIE.
THE COLORADO ROCKY MOUNTAINS.
"YOU ARE TROUBLED."
I CAN FEEL THE PAIN INSIDE YOU.
SO MUCH HAS HAPPENED SINCE...SINCE WE LAST SAW EACH OTHER. I'VE CHANGED SO MUCH...
INDEED.
I...I AM NOT THE SAME... HRIMHARI, I AM A MONSTER, A DEMON!
THE THINGS I'VE DONE...OH, GOD...WHAT I'VE DONE...

I HAVE SEEN ENOUGH OF YOUR PAIN, MY LOVE. I NEED NOT YOUR WORDS TO KNOW *YOU.*

NOTHING CAN BE THE SAME.

NOT ANYMORE. YE SHOULDN'T HAVE COME FOR ME.

YOU SAY NOTHING CAN BE THE SAME... AND I AGREE.

LOOK AT ME, RAHNE SINCLAIR.

YOU HAVE CHANGED? SO HAVE I.

I AM NO LONGER JUST THE PRINCE OF WOLVES...I AM NOW A PART OF MIDGARD AS WELL. I AM NOW PART OF YOU.

THE GODS HAVE REUNITED US FOR A REASON. AND IF THEY CAN FORGIVE YOU, YOU MUST FIND IT IN YOURSELF TO DO THE SAME.

NEW YORK CITY.
THE VANISHER IS A GIANT PIECE OF CRAP, BUT THAT BEING SAID...
...HE'S PRETTY FLAMIN' CONVENIENT.
--IS CRIMINAL! WHAT YOU'RE DOING TO ME IS WAY WORSE THAN ANYTHING I'VE DONE!!
YOU SOLD MUTANT GROWTH HORMONE TO KIDS, JACKASS.
NOT DIRECTLY. AND THEY LOVED IT!
SHUT UP, ALL OF YOU.
WE'RE HERE, SLIM. ANY UPDATES?
OUR WINDOW IS SHRINKING. GET THE KIDS OUT FAST. CABLE TAKES PRIORITY.
SO WHAT? YOUR FUTURE BUZZER GOES OFF, AND YOU JUST LET THEM DIE? IS THAT IT?
I WISH I HAD A FUTURE BUZZER. LOGAN! TELL CYCLOPS TO GET ME ONE.
THIS ISN'T A DISCUSSION, LOGAN. THIS IS EVERYTHING WE'VE BEEN FIGHTING FOR. THIS IS THE FUTURE OF MUTANTKIND.
WE'RE NOT GOING ANYWHERE UNTIL THE KIDS ARE SAFE, YOU GOT ME?
WHOA, WHAT? KIDS? WAIT... WHO EXACTLY DID THE LEPER QUEEN TAKE?
DAMMIT.

A TELEKI-WHAT?
HE CAN MOVE THINGS WITH HIS MIND.
THE ASIAN GIRL...ASHIDA... SHE CREATES ELECTRICITY...
...AND THE BLONDE CREATES SOME KIND OF ENERGY BOMBS.
JULIAN KELLER, A.K.A. HELLION.
NORIKO ASHIDA, A.K.A. SURGE.
TABITHA SMITH, A.K.A. BOOM-BOO
THEY'RE THREE OF THE MOST POWERFUL MUTANTS LEFT ON THE PLANET.
AND THEY'RE DEAD.

THIS ONE AND THE BOY, GET THEM TO THE UNITED NATIONS NOW.

WE CAN'T AFFORD THEM DETONATING BEFORE THEY REACH THE TARGET.

WHAT ABOUT THIS ONE?

GRAYMALKIN INDUSTRIES.
SCOTT...I NEED YOU IN THE LAB.
GIVE ME A MINUTE, HANK.
WE DON'T HAVE A MINUTE. I'VE FOUND CABLE.

THE SAPIEN LEAGUE. THE BOTTOM OF THE MUTANT-HATING BARREL. BUT WITH THE HELP OF BASTION THEY GOT IT TOGETHER ENOUGH TO TAG SURGE AND HELLION RIGHT UNDER OUR NOSES.

SO WHY DID PIERCE TIP THEIR HAND? WHATEVER THE REASON, IT AIN'T GONNA BE GOOD.

NO TIME FOR QUESTIONS, WE'VE GOT ***HOLES TO KILL.

DOM AND WARREN CLEAR THE PATH.

ME, JIMMY AND X GO IN.

I SHOULDN'T HAVE LET SLIP WHO THE LEPER QUEEN NABBED. JIMMY AND DOM CAN HANDLE IT, BUT FOLEY'S FREAKING OUT. AND LAURA...I COULD SMELL IT ON HER.

HER WHOLE BODY LIT UP WHEN I SAID KELLER'S NAME.
YOU GOING TO BE OKAY? YOU NEED A MINUTE?

YOU'RE DELAYING THE MISSION.
FINE. SHE'LL EITHER KEEP IT TOGETHER OR SHE WON'T. I TRIED PLAYING THE "CONCERNED LEADER..."

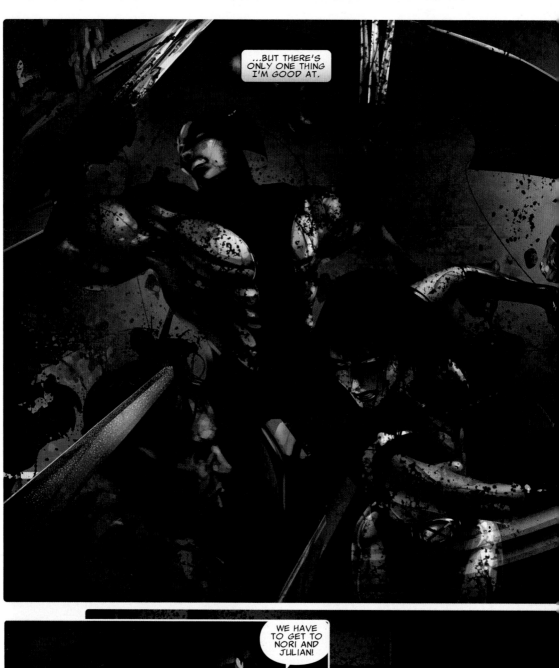

...BUT THERE'S ONLY ONE THING I'M GOOD AT.

WE HAVE TO GET TO NORI AND JULIAN!
$#&%...
YOU STAY BACK, FOLEY, DO YOU HEAR ME?
I HAVE THEIR SCENTS.

SURGE AND
ELLION HAVE
N MOVED OFF-
TE. BOOM-
OOM IS STILL
HERE.

TABBY!!

I WAS WORRIED PIERCE DIDN'T GIVE YOU OUR MESSAGE.
ONE MORE STEP, AND THE GIRL LIVES UP TO HER CODENAME.
LET HER GO!
YOU'RE DEAD, YOU KNOW THAT, RIGHT?
SAY THE WORD.
AT LEAST I DIE KILLING YOU. NOT MY OWN KIND.
LOGAN... WE FOUND CABLE.

YOU WAIT, DO YOU HEAR ME? WE'RE STILL DOWN TWO.

I'LL TAKE CARE OF THE OTHERS, BUT WE HAVE TO DO THIS NOW.

LOGAN... WHAT THE HELL ARE YOU DOING?

WE FINISH THIS MISSION...

???

COME ON...COME ON...

I'M NOT GOING TO JUST WALK AWAY FROM THEM!

NO! THE MISSION IS TO SAVE MUTANTKIND... NOTHING ELSE CAN TAKE PRIORITY, NOT EVEN THIS!!

THAT'S EXACTLY WHY IT'S NOT YOUR CALL.

DAMMIT! VANISHER, TAKE HER!

VT!

VT!

HONEY... YOU SHOULD HAVE STUCK WITH THE MASK.

RRRRAAA!!

HAND OVER THE KIDS, OR YOU'RE DEAD.

DO IT! KILL ME!!

PUSH THE BUTTON, HANK.
SCOTT...
WHERE ARE THE KIDS?!
THEY'RE DEAD! YOU'LL FIND THEIR ASHES AT THE UNITED NATIONS.
NOW KILL ME!!
NEVER MIND.
KRZZZZ

NO!!
DOM, SHOOT HER!!

FWASH!

NO...THEY WERE...THEY WERE SUPPOSED TO KILL ME...
NNN...

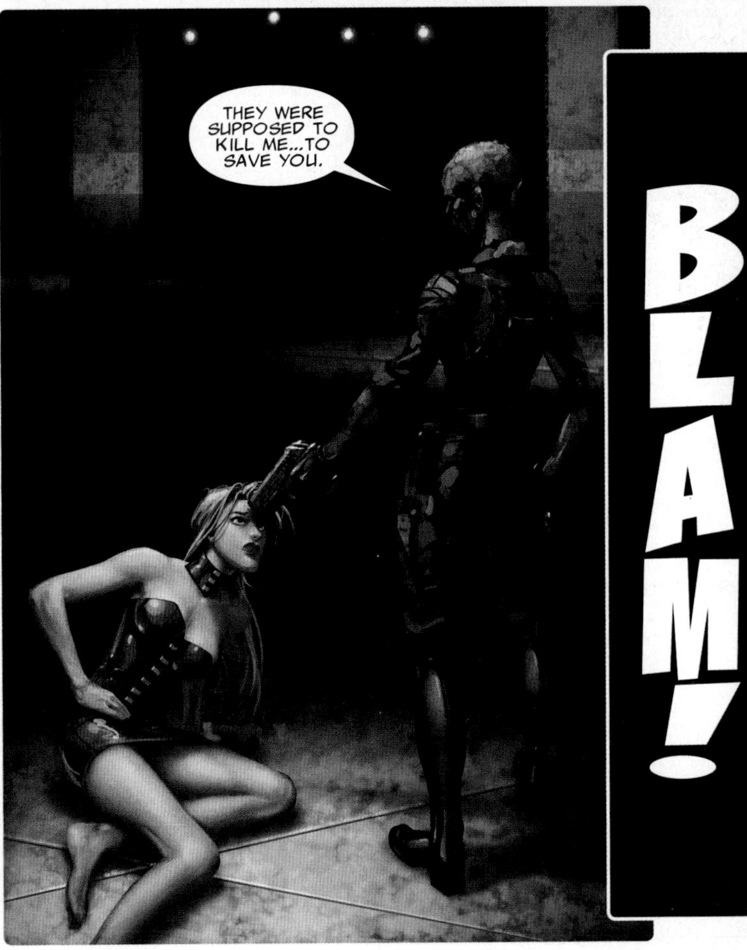
HE WON'T LET ME KILL MYSELF... BASTION WON'T LET ME DIE!
HAHAHA HA HAHAHA!! OH, GOD...PLEASE HELP ME!!
THEY WERE SUPPOSED TO KILL ME...TO SAVE YOU.
BLAM!

THEY FAILED US BOTH.
TO BE CONTINUED IN 'X-FORCE/CABLE: MESSIAH WAR'

#1 BLOODY VARIANT

#2 BLOODY VARIANT
BY CLAYTON CRAIN

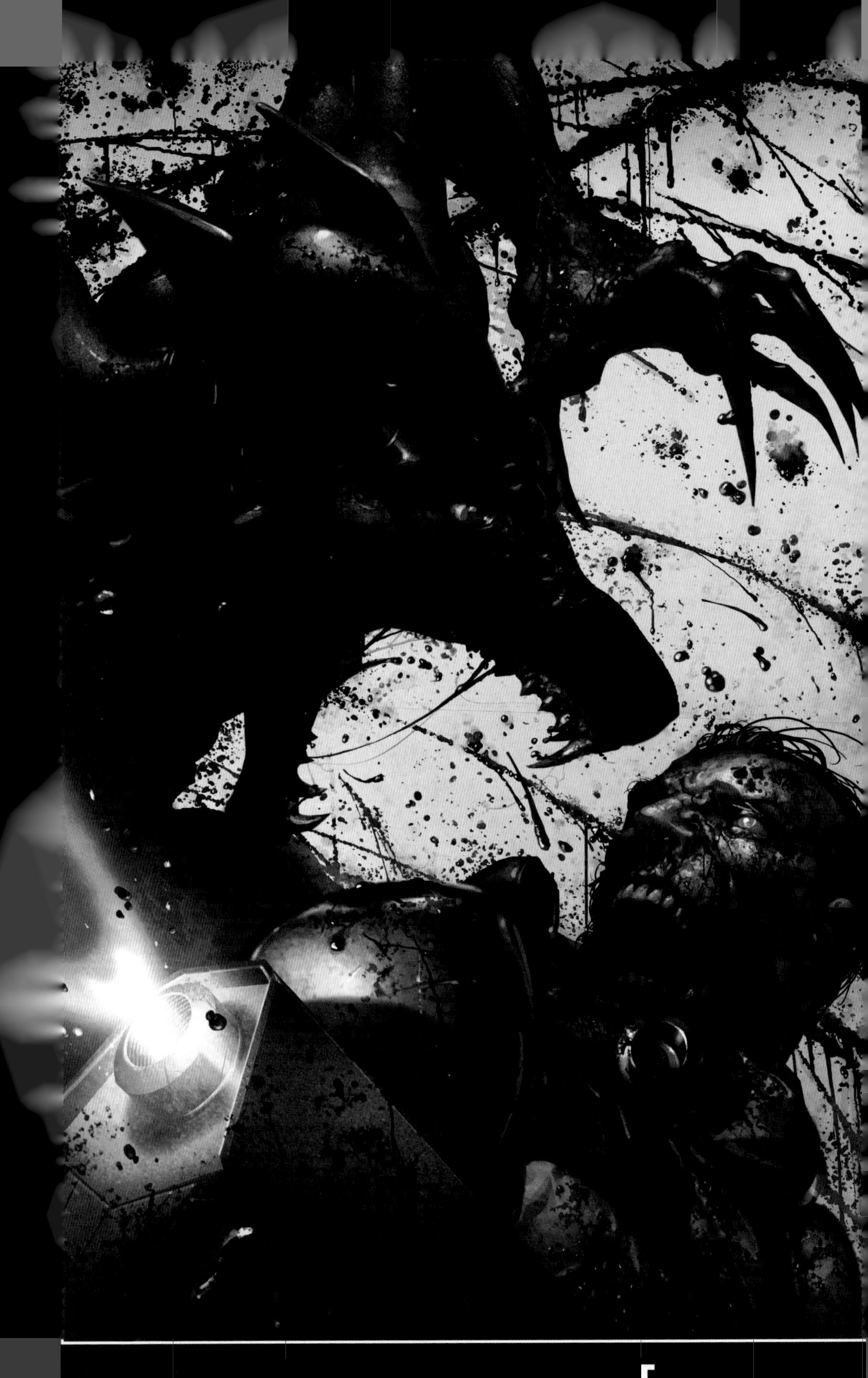

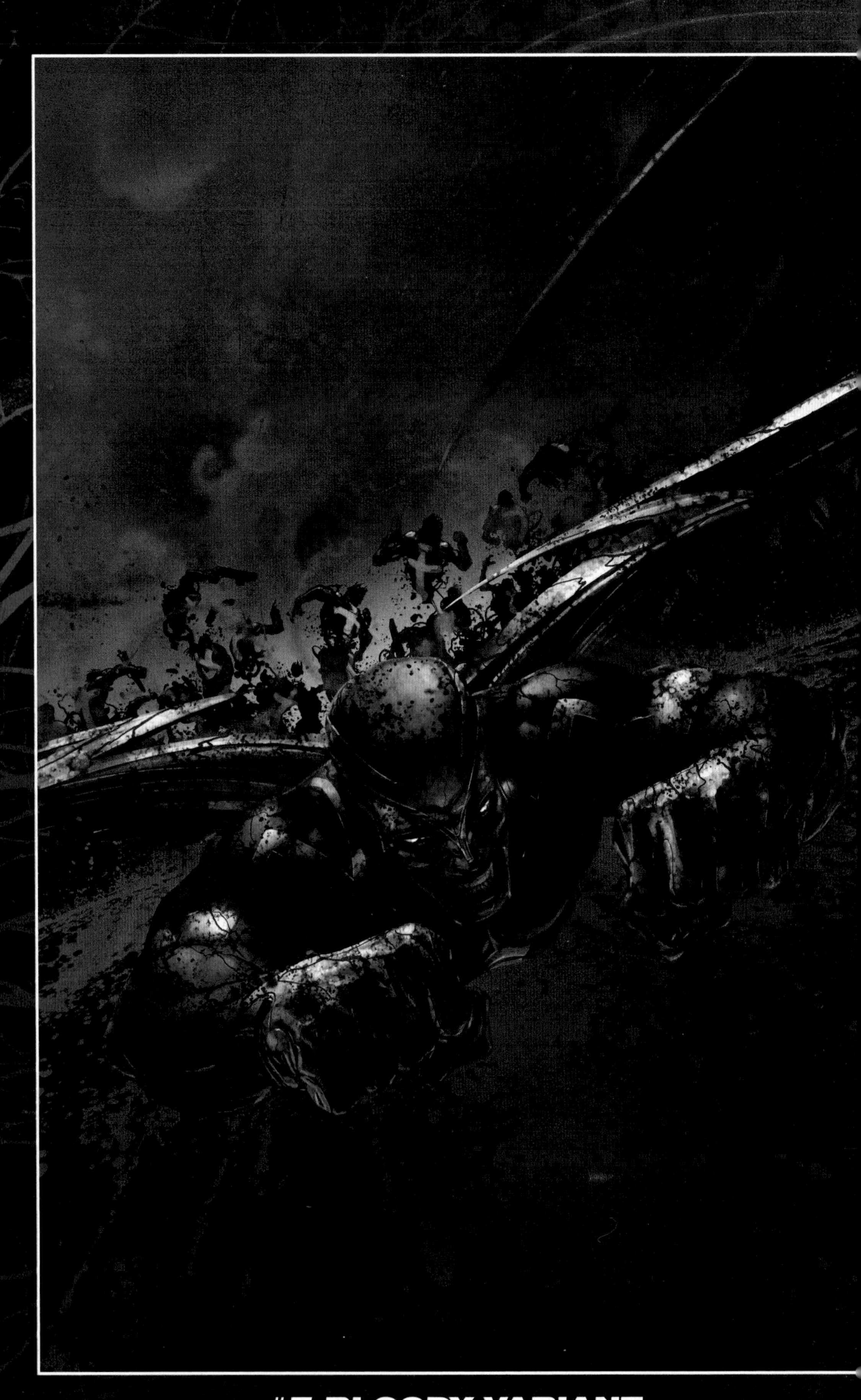

#5 BLOODY VARIANT

-FORCE: LEGACY OF VENGEANCE ONE-SHOT COVER
BY CLAYTON CRAIN

X-FORCE #7, PAGE 15

X-FORCE #8, PAGE 8

X-FORCE #8, PAGE 14

X-FORCE #9, PAGE 4

X-FORCE #9, PAGE 1